YOUR HOUSEPLANT'S FIRST YEAR

the Care & Feeding of
YOUR FIRST GROWN

DEBORAH L. MARTIN

Illustrated by YU KITO LEE

CASTLE POINT BOOKS
NEW YORK

www.castlepointbooks.com

The Castle Point Books trademark is owned by Castle Point Publishing, LLC.
Castle Point books are published and distributed by St. Martin's Publishing Group.

ISBN 978-1-250-27372-7 (paper-over-board)
ISBN 978-1-250-27373-4 (ebook)

Design by Katie Jennings Campbell
Illustrations by Yu Kito Lee

Our books may be purchased in bulk for promotional, educational, or business use.
Please contact your local bookseller or the Macmillan Corporate and
Premium Sales Department at 1-800-221-7945, extension 5442,
or by email at MacmillanSpecialMarkets@macmillan.com.

First Edition: 2021

10 9 8 7 6 5 4 3 2 1

This
plant-parenting
journey belongs to:

_____

_____

contents

WELCOME TO
PLANT PARENTHOOD

Congratulations on your new arrival!

Whether it's a bouncing begonia or a peaceful palm, your precious sprout will bring joy and quiet companionship into your life. In exchange, you will love it and give it what it needs to survive and thrive in your home.

Being a good plant parent doesn't mean lavishing your plant with the shiniest pots or the fanciest fertilizers. Successful plant parenting means being attentive to your green baby's needs and responding to those needs with consistent, loving care. Bringing up your plant doesn't require a silver trowel in its soil as much as it calls for an attentive parent who takes the time to understand its needs and to respond to its natural growth rhythms and requirements. This book will be your trusted guide on that journey.

Building the Parent-Sprout Relationship

Unlike plants growing in their natural environment or even in an outdoor garden, a plant growing indoors in a container is entirely dependent upon its human caregivers. Your sprout depends on you. Its good health and development will result from the care and guidance you provide it during its early months in your home. You naturally want to give your sprout a safe, comfortable home. That means providing shelter that is physically safe and secure, as well as one that minimizes stresses and maximizes consistency.

But your sprout also is pre-programmed by centuries of evolution to grow a certain way and to a certain size, to bloom at a particular time or in response to specific stimuli. As much as it needs your love and care, there's a lot your new sprout can do all on its own.

Give your plant secure, reliable surroundings and the conditions it needs to grow and develop according to its own natural pace. In exchange, your sprout will freshen the air around it. As you spend time caring for your own plant, you will gain a connection to the rhythms of the natural world. Raising your sprout will provide a respite from the stresses of a fast-paced, high-tech world and give you a sense of confidence in your plant-parenting abilities and pride in every achievement your green baby reaches.

Growing Stronger Together

In the pages ahead, you'll find straightforward guidance on the basics of plant parenthood: everything from lighting and potting soil, watering and feeding, to troubleshooting problems and expanding your plant family through propagation. There are also profiles of more than 100 popular houseplants to help you learn the specific needs of your own special sprout.

As your sprout grows, it may change and develop new characteristics. Its care needs may change as well, and it's up to you to adjust accordingly. Understand your sprout's needs based on its general plant type, but get to know it as an individual. Nurture its growth and change with patient, appropriate care, offering encouragement (water and fertilizer) and guidance (pruning and training) to help your own special sprout achieve its full, leafy, lovely potential.

Your plant will never wrap its leafy stems around your shoulders and thank you for the care you give it. And, if it's a cactus, that's probably a good thing! But the bond you create with your chloro-kid is real and special and an expression of the interdependence of all living things.

PART 1
THE BEST CARE BEGINS AT HOME

HELP ME GROW:
Raising Your Sprouts Right

Bringing home your own special plant may be a spur-of-the-moment act or a long-considered decision. Either way, when you step through the door with your new green baby, you experience a moment of wondering, *What's next? Now what do I do?* Whether this is your first sprout or the latest addition to a growing plant family, here are some things to consider to get your budding relationship off on the right root.

▶ *Where is baby's space?* Choose a spot that has appropriate lighting, is sheltered from drafts (hot or cold), and is where you will see and enjoy spending time with your new arrival.

▶ *Who will care for baby?* Shared parenting can be a benefit—more love for your little one! But clear communication—including setting expectations—is key. Don't leave care responsibilities to chance. Develop a schedule that identifies who will check on your leafy darling's needs and when, to reduce the risks of over- and underwatering and feeding.

▶ *What about siblings—animal, human, or plant?* Take other family members into account when choosing where to place your new sprout in your home. For the health of your green child and that of any young human or animal brothers and sisters, it's best to pick a location that minimizes sibling interactions. Your new sprout may appear defenseless, but many houseplants have toxic sap, spines, or sharp leaf edges that can pose hazards to curious kids or pets. Play it safe and teach any sentient siblings to respect their new sprout sib's boundaries, but also use physical separation for everyone's safety. Plant siblings are another matter entirely. It's great to group your new sprout with others that share similar care needs. But it makes sense to keep a new plant baby separate from established plants for a couple of weeks to make sure it hasn't brought a pest problem home with it.

PREPARING THE NURSERY

The well-equipped windowsill need not be overloaded with stuff, but you'll want to make sure it includes the right materials to nurture your sprout. Here are suggested tools and supplies, both essentials and extras, to have on hand for baby's care and support. Bear in mind that your dear leafling won't care if you water it from a repurposed sports bottle or a designer watering can, but it will very much care that you water it. Many of the items that are useful for basic plant care may be things you already have around your house or ones that are inexpensively acquired at yard sales or secondhand stores. Of course, buying for baby can be fun, too. No one is saying you can't nestle your perfect little plant child in a pretty pot that complements the colors of your drapes. But the investments your sprout will most appreciate are the ones you make in providing for its proper care.

WATERING CAN. A design with a long spout can help you put water on the potting soil surface without drenching leaves and crowns. Using a bottle with a pull-open top, such as a sports drink bottle, can also minimize drips and spills.

Shhh...🌱
Baby is
growing

THE ADJUSTMENT PERIOD

WHATEVER YOU'RE FEELING WHEN YOU ARRIVE HOME with your leafy bundle of joy, remember that change can be a traumatic experience for a plant. In nature, plants tend to live their lives in a single location. While they may grow and change over time, they rarely pick up their roots and move to an entirely different place. As a result, moving is not something that plants are evolved to do well. The change in your new plant's environment, from a warm, humid greenhouse to a warm but significantly less humid windowsill in your home, may not seem dramatic to you, but it is a big deal to your baby. Do your best to provide conditions that match preferred light levels, air temperature, and humidity. Water according to your plant's needs, but not too much. And hold off on feeding entirely until your sprout has settled in and is showing signs of new growth.

MIST/SPRAY BOTTLE. Many houseplants benefit from regular misting to increase humidity around their leaves. A spray bottle also is useful for spritzing leaves before wiping them gently to help clean off dust.

MEASURING SPOONS AND A MIXING CONTAINER. Having measuring spoons that are exclusively for use with fertilizers and any other treatments your plant might require is a good practice that avoids contaminating people food with plant chemicals. For mixing up a batch of liquid lunch for your plant's mealtime, a quart- to gallon-size container with a secure lid is nice. Then you can simply shake liquid or powder into the right volume of water.

SNIPS OR SCISSORS. For removing damaged or dying leaves and faded flowers, scissors are preferable to pulling or tearing that can damage your darling. A dedicated pair of plant-care scissors also will come in handy for taking cuttings or pruning—and will save you the trouble of searching your home for any other scissors you know are *someplace*.

SMALL TROWEL. When it's time to repot your plant, you'll want something for stirring and scooping potting soil. A trowel that is scaled down from the size useful in an outdoor garden will work. Or you can easily repurpose kitchen utensils for a variety of houseplant-care tasks: use a large spoon for soil moving, a fork for stirring granular fertilizer into the surface of potting mix, a table knife for loosening the root-ball.

LARGE PLASTIC TUB/DISHPAN. While you can repot, drench, shower, and perform other plant care in your kitchen sink or bathtub, it's much easier to have a way to contain potting soil and other messes. You're also much less likely to wind up with a drain clogged with debris. When you're not using a plastic tub to repot or water from the bottom, it can serve as storage for your sprout-care supplies.

PEBBLES AND SHALLOW TRAYS OR SAUCERS. Maintaining adequate humidity around your plant is important to its well-being. A simple, low-tech solution is to rest your plant atop a layer of pretty pebbles in a shallow tray or saucer of water. The pebbles hold your baby above the water, which evaporates and keeps baby's environment comfortable.

HUMIDIFIER. If pebble trays are not your thing, a small humidifier for baby will do nicely to keep its air pleasantly moist.

COASTERS, POT FEET, CASTORS. Plants can be messy, especially at watering and feeding time. Protect windowsills and tabletops from splashes and spills. Under baby's saucer, use a cork coaster or something similar to catch any dribbles before they leave a mark. If your sprout occupies a large pot on the floor, consider pot feet to raise it up and prevent water marks on the hardwood. A set of wheels under a large planter can be useful if you plan to move a big baby outdoors for the summer and back in for the winter.

YOU ARE MY SUNSHINE

Your little sprout needs light to perform photosynthesis, the process by which plants convert water and carbon dioxide into carbohydrates and oxygen. How much light—the hours of exposure each day and the level—has to do with your plant's natural origins. Simply put, a sweet little cactus with ancestors from a desert is going to appreciate—and need—more and brighter light than a leafy fern that traces its roots to a shady forest floor. Still, what you need to know about putting the shine in your little sunshine's life is fairly straightforward.

Satisfying Lighting Needs

All plants need light. But not all plants need exposure to the direct rays of the sun. The amount and quality of sunlight that passes through the windows of your home should guide your plant choices without preventing you from becoming a plant parent. The descriptions of plants in this book include information about the quality and quantity of light each one needs to succeed. You'll find there are houseplants suited to almost every lighting situation and ways to manage your sprout's exposure to make the most of whatever light your home has to offer.

CHECK YOUR COMPASS. The direction your windows face determines how much light shines through them for your plant's benefit. In general, south-facing windows will receive the most sunlight and are best for plants that enjoy lots of light and direct sun. Windows facing west or east may also offer your sprout direct sunlight but only for part of the day. Windows with eastern exposure typically catch the morning light, while west-facing windows get the afternoon sun. Both can meet the needs of plants that require bright light, but the sun coming in a west window tends to be more intense. If your windows face northward, they'll offer indirect light and, especially in the winter, relatively low light levels.

BRIGHT, MODERATE, OR LOW? The brightest light comes from direct rays of sunlight. For many houseplants, direct sun is too much, especially if it shines on them for several hours per day through a south-facing window. A sprout that needs bright light to put on a floral display, for example, may be happiest if it gets a few hours of direct sun in the morning, followed by bright, indirect light the rest of the time. Indirect light, such as the light a few feet from a window or to the sides, may seem bright to your eyes but it is considerably weaker than a spot in the sun. Still, most houseplants will prosper in indirect or filtered bright light, while some are able to grow happily in more modest lighting. Only a few of the plants in this book will be satisfied in low light conditions, but they are out there. Even these plants will grow more vigorously if given a bit more light to work with.

CONSIDER WINDOW TREATMENTS. Although your plant may require bright light to be its best self, filtered or dappled sunlight is the preferred choice for the majority of indoor plants, as well as for their plant parents. A sheer curtain or blinds that interrupt direct sun can let your sprout enjoy bright light while reducing the hazards of overexposure.

TAKE TIME FOR CHANGE. Dramatic changes in the quality and quantity of light your sprout receives can send it into a funk or put it at risk of sunburn. Even a plant that you might expect to enjoy full, strong sunlight may be harmed if it is suddenly placed in direct sun after growing acclimated to lower light conditions. If your sun-loving plant goes outdoors for "summer camp," for example, start it out in a shady location and move it gradually into brighter light over a period of up to 2 weeks.

SUPPLEMENTAL LIGHTING

DON'T LET A LACK OF NATURAL LIGHT in your home keep you from bringing a plant baby into your life. You may have to forgo adopting a cactus, but there are plants that will adapt to life under artificial lights. To make supplemental lighting work for your sprout, choose fluorescent or LED lights that produce light in the wavelengths that are best for plant growth. The shift from incandescent lighting to fluorescents and LEDs is good news for plant parents, because these forms of lighting are also more energy-efficient and longer-lasting while generating far less heat. To keep your baby from growing spindly as it stretches toward the light, place lighting and plants close together—about 10–12 inches.

Look Out for Leaning

Pay attention to the direction light shines on your plant and make adjustments so your baby doesn't grow lopsided. Particularly when plants are getting too little light, they will tend to bend toward the light source. Without an occasional turn of the container to give even light exposure, your sprout can develop a permanent lean. Counter the tendency to bend by turning your plant's container by a quarter turn every few days or when you water so all sides spend time "facing" toward the light.

Give Baby the Time of Its Light

Plants have evolved to use natural cues such as moisture, temperature, and light to trigger the development of their shoots, leaves, flowers, and fruits. Plants that bloom in spring, for example, are responding to increasing day length, while winter-blooming plants are prompted by decreasing amounts of daylight. Coaxing blooms from a Christmas cactus, an amaryllis, or an African violet requires making sure your sprout is getting enough nighttime rest, that is, darkness, to satisfy its "photoperiod."

Good Night, Plant

When the Light's Not Right

Diagnosing problems caused by too little or too much light can be challenging, but there are a few common hints that your plant is unhappy with its current solar situation.

▶ *Not enough*: Pale foliage, little or no new growth, failure to bloom or produce flower buds, and spindly growth that stretches toward the light are signs that your sprout is hankering for you to light up its life. Plants with colorful (variegated) foliage will tend to lose their pretty leaf markings in poor lighting.

▶ *Too much*: Pale or scorched-looking foliage with dark spots or brown leaf tips or edges is the main symptom of excessive sun exposure. Generally, plants are more able to adapt to abundant light than to too little, but ferns and others that naturally live in shady conditions are in danger of suffering sunburn in full, direct sun.

COMFY AND COZY

Your plant can't fan itself if it gets overheated nor can it put on a sweater if it feels a chill. It's up to you to make sure that conditions in your home are comfortable for your sprout. Although the most popular houseplants are those that have been chosen for their ability to live in our houses, the common methods of home heating and cooling can sometimes make life difficult for your little darling.

Indoor Air and Your Little One

While most houseplants will adapt to life at "average room temperatures," it's worth identifying the specific temperature range that's preferred by your own special sprout. A plant kept in conditions that are consistently warmer or cooler than its optimal range will be in a constant state of stress that can shorten its life and cause it to look less than its best. The closer you can come to providing your plant with the temperatures it likes best, the happier and healthier your baby will be.

GIVE TIME TO CHILL. While a plant with tropical origins may enjoy consistently warm temperatures all year round, other houseplants (including many cacti) do best if they are given a rest period, usually in winter, in cool conditions. During this time, their growth slows in response to lower light levels and they need minimal watering and fertilizing. Satisfying this need for a winter rest can be difficult when central heating makes our homes toasty and warm, but it's worth finding a cool room for your houseplant to occupy for its long-term health.

WATCH THE WATERING. Low outdoor temperatures may pose a threat to tender houseplants during the winter months, but the greater danger to your sprout can be the dry air indoors. Particularly if you keep your home cozy with forced-air heating, your leaf-baby may suffer excessive moisture loss because of the low humidity. While this takes a toll, your plant is also in peril from your good intentions. With its growth slowed in response to winter's lower lighting, it needs less water. But your baby's wilting in response to dry air triggers your parental reflex to give it a drink and, all too easily, you've overwatered it.

BOOST THE HUMIDITY. Take steps to ensure that your sprout does not dry out at any time of the year. While winter is often when houseplants are at greatest risk from overwatering, summer can be a drying time, too. Plants on the windowsill in full sun will also lose water through their foliage when the temperature soars. Provide for your sprout's humidity needs with one or more of the following methods:

▶ *Pebble tray*: Set your sprout's pot and saucer on top of a shallow tray or larger saucer containing a layer of pebbles. Pour water into the pebble tray to just cover the pebbles. As the water around the pebbles evaporates, it will moisten the air around your leafy baby. Add water to maintain moisture around the pebbles.

▶ *Share the air*: Grouping multiple houseplants with similar care needs together is a smart way to parent multiple sprouts. It can also create a microclimate of more humid air that benefits all the plants clustered together.

BABY POOL

▶ *Misting*: Treat your plant to regular spritzes with a fine-mist spray bottle to give the air around its leaves a welcome moisture boost. Use tepid water to avoid giving baby a chill and make sure your sprout doesn't mind a bit of moisture on its leaves. Furry-leaved babies like African violets are better treated to other methods of enhancing the humidity.

▶ *Humidifier*: A cool-mist humidifier can save you the effort of daily misting and the trouble of maintaining pebble trays. Place it where it will benefit your sprout and congratulate yourself for superior parenting skills.

MOVE IT. Chilly drafts and hot, dry air are definite no-no's for your little plant. But not all air movement is bad for baby. If things heat up around your sprout when the sun comes pouring in, a bit of ventilation can help to prevent heat stress. And the gently moving air around it can help your baby's leaves and stems grow stronger, too. Place a small fan where it will provide a gentle breeze and turn it on as needed, or use a timer for a daily breath of fresh air for your plant.

Beware the Danger Zones

When picking a spot for your baby's own leafy nook, be aware of potential danger zones:

▶ *Drafty areas*: Areas near doors or leaky windows put tender plants at risk of harmful chills. Some plants are able to withstand these spots, but others will drop their leaves at the first icy blast.

▶ *Heating/cooling vents*: Dry, warm air or dry, cool air blowing directly on your plant can make it uncomfortably dry. Avoid placing any plants in the path of your home's heating and air-conditioning vents.

▶ *Radiators*: The warmth of a radiator may seem like a cozy spot for a tropical plant, but the danger of drying out is very real, even if your sprout is a cactus or succulent that's fond of dry warmth. The space around a radiator can be managed for the benefit of warmth-loving plants, but it requires close monitoring to prevent your sprout from going from toasty to toasted.

▶ *Windowsill or window "chill"*: A sunny windowsill, seemingly the perfect place for happy houseplants, can pose dangers, too. On a bright winter day, the temperature can soar far beyond what is healthy for your plant, then plummet precipitously when the sun goes down. A sprout that's snug against the glass can suffer greatly in such extremes. The danger is even greater if you use curtains to cover the window at night, leaving your sprout shivering on the sill in the icy space between the glass and the curtains.

TUCK ME IN

The soil in your new sprout's pot will serve its needs in the short term while baby adjusts to life in its new home. And here's a dirty secret: your baby's pot may not contain any soil at all. For reasons of cost, weight, disease prevention, and moisture management, the nursery where your sprout was "born" very likely produces its plants in a medium made up of a few common ingredients that probably don't include actual soil. When it's time to move your plant out of the plain plastic pot it came home in and into something more decorative, you'll want to be ready with a nice potting mix to tuck its roots into.

What's in the Bag?

The contents of your little leafling's container do much more than simply hold its roots in place. True, support is one important role of a potting mix, but it also must hold water, air, and nutrients for baby's use. When you're shopping for the perfect potting medium for snuggling your sprout's roots, it's helpful to understand the ingredients in the mix so you can choose the blend that's best for your plant.

PEAT. Peat, or peat moss, is spongy plant material that comes from peat bogs found in a few unique parts of the world. Peat has excellent moisture-holding capacity and antifungal properties, so it's widely used for starting seeds and cuttings. Peat is naturally acidic, making it good for plants that require low soil pH. The peat contained in potting mediums is milled—ground to a fine texture.

SPHAGNUM. The fibrous, less decomposed, and less processed form of peat moss, sphagnum moss is springy and stringy. It features in potting mixes for orchids and bromeliads and makes a nice "nest" for epiphytes.

COIR. The shredded fibers of coconut husks, coir serves much the same purpose as peat in potting soils and is a more environmentally friendly and sustainable option.

SAND. Sand is the largest size of soil particles and is a common ingredient in potting mixtures designed for cacti and other plants that need excellent drainage.

PERLITE. What looks like polystyrene pieces in your potting medium is actually volcanic rock. It has been "popped" at a high temperature to create little fluffy bits that are full of pores for holding moisture and air. Because it is lightweight and inert, perlite is widely used to enhance drainage in potting mixes.

VERMICULITE. Another volcanic mineral that is heated to make it puff, vermiculite looks like shiny, somewhat rectangular flakes in the potting soil. Like perlite, it helps hold moisture and enhances drainage.

SOIL. Sometimes there is soil in the bag of potting soil, although it may make up only a fraction of the total ingredients. Soil is simply weathered mineral particles. Some houseplants benefit from having a bit of soil to sink their roots into and will appreciate a soil-based mix in their pot.

COMPOST OR LEAF MOLD. Decomposed organic material that contains beneficial microorganisms, compost improves drainage and moisture-holding capacity and adds modest fertility to the mix.

BARK. Composted bark is the primary ingredient of potting mediums designed for orchids. Smaller sizes of bark are used in potting soils to improve drainage.

MINERALS. Lime (a.k.a. ground limestone), gypsum, and other minerals may be added to potting mediums to balance the acidic nature of peat and to add nutrients that are gradually available for plants' use.

FERTILIZER. Many potting soils contain fertilizer, but a potting mix's physical qualities are more important to your plant's health than its fertilizer content. If you're not likely to keep up with a feeding schedule for your sprout, a potting mix with meals built in can ensure that baby gets fed, at least for a while.

WORM CASTINGS. The wastes from worms, castings are a natural, gentle fertilizer. If you buy an organic potting mix, castings may be included as the fertilizer component.

Which Bag to Grab?

Every plant parent wants the very best for their sprout, from the brightest window to the freshest water. Getting your little one into the finest potting mix matters, too. Whether you go with a national brand or a generic blend, check the label for the ingredients described above and make sure to get a product that's labeled as "potting mix," "potting medium," "potting soil," "container mix," or something of the sort. Stay away from bags that say "garden soil" or "topsoil"—these will be less pricey than potting soil and heavier, but they are no bargain. Your plant deserves a mix that's better than any old bag of dirt, or even a new bag of dirt. When shopping for potting soil, choose volume over weight, and tuck your baby into fluffy soil that will support and snuggle its roots while letting them breathe.

▶ *General-purpose mixes:* Most houseplants will prosper in a good-quality general-purpose potting mix. Some will appreciate a blend with a bit of soil in the mix, while others are happy in a soilless medium. For cacti and succulents that prefer very well-drained conditions in their containers, you can amend a general-purpose mix with sand, perlite, or vermiculite to meet their needs or buy a mix that's made with them in mind.

▶ *Specialty blends:* In addition to general-purpose potting medium, you'll also find potting mixes designed to meet the particular needs of certain types of houseplants. Blends for African violets, cacti and succulents, palms, and orchids and bromeliads offer features that will help keep these plants pleased in their pots.

Your Plant's Perfect Pot

Nearly any container that will hold potting soil may be used as a pot for your special sprout, but you'll want to make sure that baby is nestled in a planter that's practical as well as pretty. When picking a pot, you'll want to consider size and drainage first, and then factor in features such as style, color, and material.

ROOM (NOT TOO MUCH) TO GROW. Choose a container that's just right, size wise, for your sprout's roots. Avoid the temptation to move baby to a "big-kid" bed too soon. A small plant in a large pot is in danger of root rot—the excess potting soil will hold more moisture than the plant can use. Baby's first pot after the functional plastic one it came home in from the nursery should be not much bigger than what its roots will fit into. And when it's time for repotting because your sprout's roots are getting crowded or the potting soil needs to be refreshed, an increase of an inch or two in pot diameter is usually sufficient.

PLACES FOR THE WATER TO GO. Make sure baby's pot has holes for drainage so that water doesn't pool around its roots. If you have a pretty planter picked out to match your home décor and it lacks proper drainage, use it as holder (called a cachepot) for a more practical container. Put a layer of pebbles in the bottom of the outer, decorative pot, then rest baby's functional container atop them. When you water, make sure the bottom of your sprout's true home is above the level of any water that runs through into the cachepot. Remember drainage when you're putting your baby's planter in its place in your home—a saucer or other water-catching accessory is a must to protect your furnishings from drips and dribbles.

MADE OF THE RIGHT STUFF. The material your sprout's pot is made of will affect how quickly its potting soil dries out between waterings and can play a role in temperature, too. Clay, or terra-cotta, containers are porous and so dry out faster than plastic or glass or even glazed ceramic pots. This can help keep baby healthy and prevent the problems caused by soggy soil, but it also means you need to be more attentive to meeting watering needs.

TIPPING THE SCALES. If your special plant is a statuesque sprout, you'll want to consider the weight of the container you choose. Tall plants can be top-heavy and in danger of tipping over if they're not balanced at the base with a heavy pot to hold them. But if your leaf baby is more inclined to vine and swing from a hanging basket, you'll want a container that's light and less likely to pull its supporting hardware out of your wall.

THE EFFECTS OF COLOR. Apart from coordinating with your home's décor, the color of your sprout's container can affect the temperature of its root zone. This may not matter if your baby spends all its time indoors and out of direct sunlight, but a sprout that goes outside for the summer or one that rests in a sunny spot needs to be safeguarded from overheating. A dark-colored pot will absorb sunlight, causing temperatures in the root zone to grow uncomfortably warm and also drying the plant out more quickly than you might expect.

Nourishing Healthy Plants

As a proud plant parent, you'll want to make sure to shower your leafy little one with all the liquid love and balanced nutrition it requires. But more is not always better. Part of your responsible care is to know the signs that your plant needs a drink or nourishment—or doesn't. Don't worry: it's not as tricky as it sounds. If you're attentive, you'll learn your plant's needs and signals that it's not getting all the keys to growing at its best. Rely on the information you're storing up now and your plant-parent instincts, and you'll both thrive.

WETTING YOUR PLANTS

While getting your plant on a regular watering schedule may be helpful to you, it's more important that you learn the signs that indicate your sprout is getting too much or too little of the moisture it needs. Because it can't tell you in words when it's thirsty—or drowning—it's up to you to become familiar with your plant's general water requirements and to develop a watering routine based on your youngster's stage of growth and the conditions created by its location in your home.

What's Best for Baby

Almost as important as the quantity of water you provide for your plant is the quality of that water. Depending on the source of the water that comes from the tap in your home, it may require some preparation before you pour it into your baby's pot.

AVOID THE MUNICIPAL TREATMENT. Chlorine and fluoride are chemicals that often are added to municipal water supplies. The former is used to kill pathogens in our drinking water and the latter is added to promote healthy teeth. These things are generally good for humans who drink the water but not great for plants. Both can cause leaf burn in houseplants and also may reduce flowering in blooming plants. Fluoride causes a condition known as fluoride tip burn in susceptible species, such as spider plants and dracaenas, in which the tips of the leaves turn an unattractive brown and dry up and crumble. If your water smells of chlorine—which sometimes happens during rainy seasons when the treatment facility is addressing overabundant supplies—fill an open container with water and let it stand overnight to allow the chlorine to dissipate as a gas.

WELL, WELL, WELL. If the water in your home comes from a well, it may contain dissolved minerals such as calcium and magnesium that are good for you but too much for many houseplants. If you know your water is hard, running it through a basic carbon filter will make it better for your plant babies.

DON'T GO SOFT. Water that has been chemically softened to remove its mineral content is too salty for your plants. The salts used to make water "soft" will alter the pH of the soil in their pots and interfere with their ability to take up nutrients and water. If you can't divert water from your home system before it goes through the water softener, get the water for your plants from another source.

MAKE IT RAIN. Collecting rainwater (or melting snow) for your family plants is an act of love that can save them from the typically hard water that comes from the tap, as well as a means of avoiding chemicals added at the local municipal water plant.

BOTTLED OR TAP? There's no need to serve your precious plants fancy imported bottled water. But what's good for you is good for baby—if you're filtering your water for your own use, go ahead and use filtered water for your plants. Distilled water is also a good choice for keeping baby properly hydrated without icky additives.

Timing and Temperature

Everything from your chosen pot to the time of year and the temperature and humidity in your home will determine how much and how often your precious plant will need water. Once you understand your baby's basic requirements, monitor its soil regularly to see how long it takes to dry out. Some plants prefer steadily moist soil, while others need the top half to 1 inch of their potting mix to dry out between waterings. *Very few houseplants do well in soggy conditions.*

YOU KNOW BABY BEST

While moisture probes and other devices can help tell you when to water, your own observations often are a more reliable way to make that call. Poke a finger into the potting soil and feel for yourself. If you can't easily stick your finger into the soil because of low-growing leaves that cover the surface, use weight to help guide your assessment—if the pot feels unusually light when you lift it, chances are the contents are very dry.

REMEMBER THAT BABY CRAVES CONSISTENCY. Avoid extremes of wet or dry soil, as both can cause serious harm. Try not to let your plant's soil dry out completely–potting mixes can be notoriously difficult to rewet. At the other end of the spectrum, overwatering is the main cause of houseplant demise. Roots need oxygen as well as water and soil that is waterlogged causes roots to die and rot.

NOT TOO HOT, NOT TOO COLD. When it is time for a drink, give baby water that is comfortably room temperature. Very hot water is a no-no for obvious reasons, but chilly liquid can shock your baby's roots and cause unsightly spotting on leaves.

When Baby Wants a Drink

No sippy cup is needed for giving your plant water, but you may want some specialized watering tools and strategies to help deliver the liquid where it's meant to go. A watering can with a long, narrow spout makes it easier to pour water onto the surface of the soil in a plant's pot while avoiding splashing its leaves. And a saucer is useful for watering a pot from the bottom, a practical technique for letting your sprout soak up water without getting too much around its leaves and stems.

TAKE IT FROM THE TOP. Watering from above may seem like you're doing it the way nature intended. But plants that are sheltered from the other conditions found outdoors–wind, sunlight, changing temperatures–won't dry off as quickly after a rain simulation. Apply water to the top of the soil in your plant's pot and pour until it starts to run out through the drainage holes in the bottom.

BOTTOMS UP. Watering from below is a good way to hydrate fuzzy-leaved babes like African violets and others that dislike getting water on their leaves. This method is also helpful when your bushy baby's foliage covers the surface of the soil in its pot, making it difficult for you to pour water in without it running off the leaves. Set your plant's pot in a saucer of tepid water and let it drink through its drainage holes for no more than 30 minutes at a time.

TIDY UP THE AFTER-BATH. Don't leave water standing in the saucer after your baby has had its drink. Soggy soil is a definite danger to plant health. Pour off the extra water.

FEEDING TIME

Plants (even carnivorous ones!) "eat" their food in liquid form, absorbing it through their roots or, sometimes, through pores in their foliage. Although fertilizers come in many forms— concentrated liquids, powders to be dissolved in water, or granules to be sprinkled over the soil surface or stirred into the potting mix, to name a few—all types are absorbed by your plant's roots when they are in solution in the water you supply.

A new arrival, fresh from the nursery, may come to you with fertilizer already enriching the potting soil in its container. Look for colorful rounded pellets of slow-release fertilizer, often green or yellow, on the surface of the soil in your plant's pot. This is a good sign that your baby's nutritional needs have been taken care of before you brought it into your family. Even if you don't see evidence of fertilizer, most commercial potting soils have fertilizer in them. For this, and other reasons, it's best to wait awhile before introducing fertilizer to your new sprout's care regimen.

What Time Is Dinner?

As you've already learned, change can be stressful to your plant. While it's tempting to shower your sprout with all kinds of signs of your affection the moment it comes into your home, it needs time to settle in. Keep your new arrival on a water-only diet while it becomes accustomed to the conditions in its new surroundings.

Base further decisions about when to start supplementing water with nutrients on your little one's specific needs and on the time of year and stage of growth. Slow-growing plants, for example, have modest fertilizer needs but will benefit from nourishment provided in spring at the start of the active growth period for most houseplants. If your baby is known for beautiful blooms, you'll want to plan its meals to support the development of buds and flowers. And nearly all houseplants need less feeding in winter when low light levels and cooler temperatures contribute to slower growth. The profiles in this book provide information about the feeding needs of the plants described.

Understanding Nutritional Needs

Although your plant already knows how to make its own food via photosynthesis (of course it does—it's a prodigy!), baby can't live on carbs alone. Three main nutrients are essential for healthy plant growth. They are nitrogen (N), phosphorus (P), and potassium (K), identified by their abbreviations from the periodic table of elements and corresponding to the three numbers found on almost every fertilizer product label.

You can be a successful plant parent without digging too deeply into the chemistry of plant fertilizers. But it helps to understand a little bit about how plants use the three major nutrients so you can provide your own special sprout with a diet that matches its developmental needs.

NITROGEN. Plants need nitrogen to support healthy leaf, shoot, and stem growth and to produce chlorophyll, a key ingredient in photosynthesis. Too little nitrogen can leave plants stunted and pale; too much can burn plant tissues or encourage lush, floppy growth that is prone to disease and attractive to pests. All plants need nitrogen, but those grown for their foliage may benefit from fertilizers that have more nitrogen relative to the other ingredients.

PHOSPHORUS. Flowers, fruits, and roots all depend on an adequate supply of phosphorus. In the vegetable garden, tomatoes, peppers, and carrots are among the crops that appreciate fertilizers that favor phosphorus over nitrogen. Flowering and fruiting houseplants and bulbs can benefit from such formulas, too.

POTASSIUM. Represented by the third number on a fertilizer label and abbreviated K, potassium helps plants regulate their moisture uptake and the exchange of gases through the pores in their leaves.

OTHER GOODIES

Micronutrients are things like calcium, iron, and magnesium that plants need in small quantities. Some plants require specific micronutrients in their diet. Many micronutrients are naturally present in potting soil, but may be depleted over time and must be replenished through fertilizing.

AN ALL-NATURAL DIET

You'll find plenty of houseplant fertilizer products derived from organic materials to nurture your little flower child. While fertilizers labeled as "natural" or "organic" generally contain lower concentrations of the three major nutrients when compared with synthetic products, they frequently include more of the micronutrients and beneficial microorganisms your baby needs. But your plant is unlikely to turn up its roots at any meal you offer it, as long as you're providing the nutrients it needs, when it needs them.

What to Serve

A "balanced" plant food is one that contains equal percentages of the three major plant nutrients. Its label might carry numbers like 10-10-10. If you are parent to a brood of houseplants, a balanced fertilizer offers the convenience of being a dish the whole family can enjoy. Or you can choose a food for your sprout that is tailored to its particular needs and talents. For example, your fiddle-leaf fig will enjoy a meal that includes more nitrogen, such as 10-5-5, to help it maintain those big glossy leaves. If your baby is a beautiful bloomer like a Christmas cactus, you might serve it something with more phosphorus (5-10-5.) to encourage a healthy floral display.

The different formulations of fertilizer may be offered as "foliage plant" or "flowering plant" fertilizer, and you may also find foods customized for African violets, cacti, orchids, or other related groups. These specialized diets can take the worry out of feeding your sprout by helping to ensure that you're satisfying its particular nutritional needs.

LIQUID OR SOLID. Fertilizers may be liquid, granular, encapsulated, or solid—such as spikes made to stick into the soil for gradual release. The form you choose for feeding your sprouts may be largely a matter of convenience. A liquid that can be served when you water your baby makes mealtime quick and easy. Granular fertilizers typically are scratched into the surface of your sprout's potting soil. Time-release fertilizers have coatings that break down gradually, delivering meals to your plant over an extended period with little parental involvement. This is true of fertilizer spikes as well, but with the caveat that these may deliver nourishment unevenly.

HOW OFTEN TO FEED. While watering your plant should be responsive to its individual preferences, you can establish a schedule for fertilizing based on baby's general nutritional needs and the time of year. As a rule, feeding your little green ones is most important during times when they are actively growing. While you may think of your plants as growing year-round, many houseplants take a winter rest when low light levels and cooler temperatures prompt them to slow down for a few months. During this nap time, your sprout needs less water and less—maybe even no—food. From spring into fall, follow a meal schedule that matches your sprout's growth patterns and needs. You'll find suggestions for feeding routines in the plant profiles.

HOW MUCH IS TOO MUCH? Like overwatering, overfeeding poses serious risks to your sprout's health. No matter what your grandmother told you, food is not love when it comes to your plant and more is not better. Overfeeding can make your plant a target for pest and disease problems, and excess fertilizer can build up in the potting medium and burn its tender roots. Use the guidance in the plant profiles and your own observations to develop a feeding routine and stick to it. Don't be tempted to react to signs of distress by dosing your little one with fertilizer. Unless you are certain that your sprout needs feeding— and this can be hard to distinguish from other problems—hold off on fertilizing a plant in distress. A sprout that is struggling needs to regain its basic health before it is prepared to get growing once more. See "Clues to Sprout Symptoms" on pages 36–37 for a checklist to review when your little one seems out of sorts.

Postmeal Cleanup

No matter how tidy your plant looks, it is likely a little bit of a messy eater. Its roots are bound to leave a few "morsels" of fertilizer behind after every meal. Over time, those bits of plant food accumulate on the sides of your plant's container, in the form of salts, which may appear as a light-colored residue around the inner rim of the pot, usually at and just above the soil level. Besides looking unsightly, the buildup of salts in the container can harm your little one's roots, reducing its ability to take up the water and nutrients it needs to grow happy and healthy.

Before any harm results from a too-salty situation, take measures to wash away those plant-food leftovers with a thorough drenching of your sprout's root zone. Two to four times per year, water your plant with a copious drink of fresh, room-temperature water. Let the container drain for a half hour, then pour your baby another one. After the excess from the second drenching drink has drained off, return your baby to its proper place and wait for things to dry out accordingly before offering it more to eat or drink.

LOVE ME:
Wellness Checks and Milestones

Enjoy the benefits of being a plant parent and keep your sprout happy and healthy. Spend time together, even just a few minutes every day as you get to know your plant's habits and needs. With a daily check-in you will develop a feel for how often baby needs water, you'll notice those precious first new leaves or flowers, you'll see if there are signs of trouble or hints that your little one is ready for a new container. As you gain confidence in your plant-parenting skills, you and your sprout will settle into a comfortable routine, secure in your connection with each other.

PRACTICE GOOD GROOMING

First Haircut

Keeping your sprout looking its best will give you a chance to monitor its health and spot any problems before they get out of hand. Make a regular date with your sprout once every week or two to groom it and check for signs of healthy growth or matters of concern. Customize your care to your little one's personality—gently wipe broad, glossy leaves like those of a fiddle-leaf fig or philodendron with a damp cloth to clean them. Use a soft paintbrush to dust off the fuzzy foliage of African violets or to clean between the spines of a cactus. Rinse palms, ferns, and others with lots of little leaves with an occasional gentle shower—just make sure the water is tepid and that any excess water drains off after the bath.

Use scissors to remove faded flowers and damaged or declining leaves. Resist the temptation to pinch or pull off old foliage or wilted blooms with your fingers; it's too easy to accidentally twist or break a stem or pull too hard and damage your baby's roots.

Go ahead and talk to your sprout as you tidy it up. Your talented leaf baby will turn the carbon dioxide from your breath into oxygen!

HUNGRY OR THIRSTY?

JUST AS PEOPLE CAN MISTAKE THIRST FOR HUNGER and overeat as a result, feeding your plant when its soil is too dry can cause it to gobble up too many nutrients all at once. Your darling sprout won't get fat, but it can suffer ill effects from overfeeding. If your baby's watering routine gets out of whack and you find it looking thirsty, focus on rehydration first and serve its next meal only after the soil in its pot is once again appropriately moistened.

WATCH FOR SIGNS OF TROUBLE

During your grooming sessions, give your sprout a thorough once-over. Regular monitoring makes it more likely that you'll spot any causes for concern before things get out of hand. Although your plant can't talk, it likely will show you when something's wrong and it's counting on you to read its signals. This is why it's so important to spend a little time every day checking on your plant—so you will be quick to see when something changes that needs your attention.

WHAT'S WRONG? Unfortunately, your sprout has a limited "vocabulary" to tell you what's troubling it, and many different problems can produce almost identical symptoms. Wilting, for example, can result from underwatering or overwatering or too much heat or sunlight, or it may indicate overcrowded roots in need of a bigger pot. Knowing your own special sprout's care requirements—its preferred temperature and humidity levels, how much light it needs, how often it needs to be watered and fed—can help you rule out many causes when a problem occurs.

BE CONSISTENT. Steady, appropriate care is the best protection you can give your baby against almost every threat to its health. The stress caused by erratic watering, too-dry air, exposure to drafts or overheating, and other lapses in care can make a plant more susceptible to diseases and more attractive to pests.

START WITH THE BASICS. When you spot a limp leaf or a drooping stem that seems cause for concern, review baby's care and location before you leap to conclude that your darling is under attack by pests or afflicted with a dire disease. It may take only a simple change—moving baby out of the hot sun or watering more thoroughly but less often—to restore your sprout's health.

Clues to Sprout Symptoms

Diagnosing what's wrong with your plant can be tricky at best. This table lists common symptoms and possible causes, to help you decide what to do when baby is in distress.

Leaf Symptoms	May be caused by
PALE OR YELLOW LEAVES	▶ Over- or underwatering ▶ Lack of feeding; may also have darker veins and pale surfaces between veins ▶ Too little light ▶ Sunburn; succulents may turn reddish ▶ Exposure to cold drafts ▶ Natural shedding of leaves (if mainly older, lower leaves being lost)
DARK GREEN, CURLED LEAVES	▶ Overfeeding ▶ Too warm ▶ Pests
BROWN TIPS OR EDGES	▶ Under- or overwatering ▶ Dry air ▶ Fluoride or chlorine in water ▶ Overheating, too much direct sun ▶ Overfeeding
DARK SPOTS	▶ Sunburn, scorch ▶ Overwatering (spots), underwatering (dry patches) ▶ Fungal leaf spot (spots have obvious margins, sunken centers) ▶ Scale insects (raised bumps)
LIGHT SPOTS	▶ Hard or cold water on leaves ▶ Spider mites (pale, stippled spots)
HOLES IN LEAVES	▶ Pests ▶ Curious pets or careless people
EXCESSIVE LEAF LOSS	▶ Environmental stress; recent change ▶ Pests ▶ Root rot
POWDERY COATING ON SURFACE	▶ Fungal infection
DARK, SHINY, STICKY COATING ON SURFACE	▶ Sooty mold growing on "honeydew" excreted by pests

Flower Symptoms	May be caused by
BUDS DROP BEFORE OPENING	▶ Environmental stress; recent change ▶ Dry air ▶ Over- or underwatering ▶ Too cold or warm ▶ Pests
NO BUDS OR FLOWERS FORM	▶ Insufficient light ▶ Too much nitrogen fertilizer ▶ Too little phosphorus fertilizer ▶ Low humidity; underwatering ▶ Container is too big

Root Symptoms	May be caused by
ROOTS GROWING OUT DRAINAGE HOLES	▶ Overcrowded roots, a.k.a. pot-bound or root-bound
FINE, NETLIKE ROOTS ON TOP OF POTTING MIX	▶ Overcrowded roots, a.k.a. pot-bound or root-bound
ROOTS CIRCLING AROUND SIDES OF POT	▶ Overcrowded roots, a.k.a. pot-bound or root=bound
DARK/BLACKENED, MUSHY ROOTS	▶ Root rot disease, promoted by overwatering

Whole Plant Symptoms	May be caused by
WEAK OR LITTLE TO NO NEW GROWTH	▶ Too-little fertilizer ▶ Container is too small; roots constricted
TALL, PALE, SPINDLY GROWTH	▶ Insufficient light
OVERALL WILTING	▶ Under- or overwatering ▶ Pests or disease at roots
MOLD OR FUZZY GROWTH	▶ Fungal disease
BLACKENED, MUSHY STEMS	▶ Root rot, a.k.a. crown rot

Solving Common Pest and Disease Problems Safely

Pest problems in houseplants are not particularly common. Most often an
infestation occurs when pests come into the house on a newly purchased plant
or when plants have spent time outdoors and carry pests back in with them
in the fall. By regularly monitoring and grooming leaf babies, you'll be likely
to spot any creepy-crawlies before they overrun your houseplants. Then, take
speedy action to put a stop to invading pests.

▶ *Separate siblings*: Isolate an infested
plant from any pest-free plants to
prevent problems from spreading.

▶ *Focus on safety*: Use the least-toxic
method of quelling the pest problem
(see the tips in the chart on pages
39–40), then continue to keep the
patient separate from the rest of your
plant family until you're sure the pests
are vanquished.

Pest	What you see	What to do
APHIDS	Tiny, pear-shaped, pale green or black insects, often numerous and clustered on buds, shoots, under leaves, and at leaf axils. Affected areas may be distorted, sticky with honeydew, and blackened (see Sooty mold).	Wash aphids from your plants with a spray of water; crush them with gloved fingers and wipe away with a damp cloth. If they persist, use insecticidal soap spray.
FUNGUS GNATS	Small, gray flying insects that hang around moist potting mix; larvae are white maggots found in the soil. Mostly an annoyance around seedling flats; occasionally pesky in terrariums.	Use a yellow sticky trap in the pot of infested plants. Change potting soil and improve ventilation to discourage these pests.
MEALYBUGS	Looking like bits of white fluff clustered at the base of leaves and stems, they suck plant juices and secrete honeydew; sooty mold may appear.	Wipe them away and treat with mild soap spray or use a cotton swab dipped in alcohol to wipe them off.
SCALE INSECTS	Dark-colored bumps on stems and under leaves, scales are rather common on palms and can be hard to control because of their waxy coverings. They secrete sticky honeydew, which may support sooty mold. A severe infestation of scale may mean getting rid of the affected plant.	If just a few are present, scrape them carefully from your plant. Remove heavily infested branches. Use a cotton swab to dab with rubbing alcohol.
SPIDER MITES	Tiny red moving pinpoints and webbing on leaves, stems, and buds. Infested plants may have pale, stippled leaves where mites are feeding. Hold a sheet of paper under affected plants and shake them to see if mites are visible on the paper.	Remove heavily affected plant parts. Wash mites from plants with a sprayer or under the shower. They are most often a problem in dry air; increasing humidity and misting plants can help prevent recurring infestation. Soap spray may also be used.
WHITEFLY	Tiny but very visible white flying insects that rise up in clouds when disturbed. They suck plant juices and secrete honeydew and reduce the vigor of plants they infest.	Use yellow sticky traps in or near infested plants. Spray with insecticidal soap.

Disease	What you see	What to do?
FUNGAL LEAF SPOT	Dark spots with distinct, yellow margins and sunken centers	Remove affected leaves. Increase airflow around your plant; water and feed appropriately.
POWDERY MILDEW	White, powdery coating on leaves; often appears when plants suffer from moisture stress and poor air movement.	Remove affected foliage. Water well and strive to maintain soil moisture while increasing ventilation.
ROOT ROT, CROWN ROT	You may not see this until it's too late. Plants that wilt and don't recover with watering may be afflicted. Remove the plant from its pot and look for blackened, mushy roots or for similar symptoms at soil level of low-growing plants. If decay is extensive, discard the entire plant.	Avoid overwatering and prolonged soggy conditions that promote root rot. If only a few roots are affected, cut them off and repot the plant in fresh potting mix.
SOOTY MOLD	Black, dusty-looking coating on leaves and stems that forms on shiny, sticky honeydew produced by various sucking insects. Unsightly and reduces plant health by blocking light absorption.	Treat the pest problem and wipe away sooty mold with damp cloth; remove severely affected parts.

GROWING UP SO FAST

When your sprout begins to show signs of being cramped in its pot, it's time to give it more room to stretch its roots. Repotting (or potting up), the plant-parenting equivalent of moving from a crib to a big-kid bed, is called for when your sprout starts sticking its roots out of the drainage hole, when roots are congested on the outer surface of the root-ball when you peek into the pot, or when wilting and pale leaves indicate your plant's roots are constricted and not able to take up water and nutrients to support the foliage.

Repotting is not just for plants that are pot-bound, though. Over time, the potting soil in a container becomes worn out. The minerals are depleted and organic matter breaks down, resulting in low fertility and shrinking pore spaces for holding moisture, air, and nutrients for your sprout's roots to enjoy. Even if your container remains a suitable size, repotting every couple of years to refresh the potting mix is beneficial for your plant's health.

Once your little one grows to a not-so-little size, repotting may become a challenge. Plants in large, heavy pots may be refreshed by carefully removing the top layer of the soil in their containers, adding a serving of slow-release fertilizer, then adding fresh potting medium to the same depth as the old soil. Do this every spring for your big babies to keep them happy and healthy.

Repotting Step-by-Step

Repot in the spring or early summer to take advantage of your sprout's active growth period. Some plants get a little sulky after their roots are disturbed, so timing is important to help them bounce back quickly.

1. Water your plant a day before you plan to repot it, and assemble your materials: a new pot in the appropriate size, fresh potting soil, and a protected work surface. It can be helpful to have a pair of scissors or pruning shears on hand, in case trimming needs become apparent while you're working.

2. Moisten the new potting soil and put about an inch of fresh potting soil in the bottom of your baby's pot-to-be.

3. Tip the container and knock the sides (flex the sides of plastic pots) to loosen any clinging roots. Place your palm on top of the soil in the pot with your fingers on either side of your sprout's crown or main stem, and tip the plant and root-ball out onto your supporting hand. If it resists leaving the pot, run a table knife around the inside of the pot to help it release. *Avoid pulling on the stem(s) and leaves*; the goal is to slide the root-ball gently from the pot without harming your plant.

4. While its root-ball is out of the pot, examine baby's roots and tidy them up if needed. Gently tease out crowded roots and use the scissors to trim off very long circling roots. If there are signs of decay—blackened or dark, mushy

roots—prune these back to light, healthy growth. You can snip your sprout's roots back by about one-fourth of their total without fear; most plants will respond with healthy new root growth in their refreshed container.

5. Set your sprout into the new pot, supporting it at the same depth it occupied in its previous quarters. Fill in around it with fresh, moistened potting soil, tucking its roots into the new container and pressing the mix in gently to ensure good contact between roots and soil. Tap the container firmly to settle the mix and top off to within about an inch of the pot rim.

6. If you've planted in moistened potting medium, hold off for a day or two before giving your baby a drink. Watch for signs of settling that indicate gaps beneath the potting soil's surface and fill in as needed. Continue to provide your plant the care and love it needs and watch it thrive in its new container.

EXPANDING THE FAMILY

Propagation refers to all the ways in which new plants are created, from seeds to cuttings to offsets to laboratory tissue culture. Some houseplants (spider plants, for example) are almost ridiculously easy to propagate, while others (such as orchids) can be difficult to replicate without painstaking techniques. In the plant descriptions in Part 2, you'll find preferred propagation methods mentioned for those houseplants that lend themselves to simple reproduction and/or for those that benefit from being propagated.

BiG SiSTER

LiTTLE SiSTER

Propagation can be a fun activity for you and your sprout to share. Perhaps your little one is begging you for siblings to keep it company while you're at work. You may want to spread the joy of plant parenting among your friends and family by gifting them with copies of your little leafling to raise as their own. Or propagation may be a way to extend the time you have with your sprout—some plants decline or grow unattractive with age and are best started anew from a cutting or offshoot of the original.

Making Copies

Cuttings, offshoots, and divisions all are asexual methods of reproducing plants, meaning they happen without any floral parts, pollination, or seeds. The new plants that result from asexual propagation are genetic copies of the parent plant. Even if your firstborn becomes a leggy, scraggly teenager that eventually outgrows its space in your home, it can live on as an adorable cutting, refreshed and ready to receive your loving care.

Propagation Basics

Increasing your plant family can be fun and rewarding. While the techniques described here are simple and don't require any specialized tools, it's helpful to have a few items on hand to make the process go smoothly.

▶ Sharp scissors or knife for taking cuttings

▶ Seed-starting or other soilless potting mix

▶ Plastic pots or trays, small jars for rooting in water

▶ Watering can with a rose attachment for gentle sprinkling

▶ Plastic bags and rubber bands for covering pots of cuttings to maintain humidity

▶ Rooting hormone powder (optional, but helpful for plants that are slow to develop roots from cuttings)

Simple Propagation How-Tos

As with repotting, the best time to propagate your plant is in spring or early summer when new growth is naturally occurring.

STEM CUTTINGS. Take cuttings from young, healthy growth. Using sharp scissors or a knife, cut off a 4- to 6-inch tip of a non-flowering stem, removing it just below a leaf axil. Remove the lower leaves from the cutting, then dip the cut end in rooting hormone powder, if using. Prepare a container with premoistened seed-starting or soilless mix and use your finger or a pencil to make a hole in the medium. Stick the end of the cutting into the medium and gently firm the mix around the cutting. Water lightly. Cover the container with a tented plastic bag to hold in moisture; secure with a rubber band if needed. Put the container in a bright spot out of direct sun. Keep the potting mix moist but not soggy. Within 6 to 8 weeks, roots should develop.

EASY TO ROOT IN WATER. Cuttings of some plants will root readily in water. Take a cutting as described above or of a leaf and attached stem and stick it into a small jar of water, keeping all foliage above the water. Rooting should take place within a few weeks; you may need to add water or refresh the water while you wait. Once several roots have grown, move the new plant into a container of potting soil. Among the plants that root easily in water are African violet, pothos, pilea, and inch plant.

LEAF CUTTINGS. A few houseplants are able to develop roots from their leaves, a nifty trick that's useful for propagating showy begonias as well as some succulents and cacti. To make cuttings from a begonia leaf, clip off a large, healthy leaf at the base of its stem. Remove the central part of the leaf where the stem is attached and cut the remaining leaf blade into 1-inch sections with visible veins running to the cut edge. Tuck these leaf sections into the surface of a pot of moist potting mix so they are upright with the veins contacting the medium. Gently firm the mix around them and cover the pot to hold in moisture. Watch for small plants to form at the veins, usually within 2 months, at which time you can move them into pots of their own. Root entire leaves of succulents or pads of cacti, allowing the cut surfaces to dry overnight before sticking them in a moist cactus potting mix.

DIVISIONS. Plants with fibrous roots and multiple crowns or shoots can often be propagated by separating them into clumps of roots and stems. This method works well for plants such as Boston ferns and peace lilies. Water the plant ahead of time to make it easier to work with. Remove it from its pot and gently pull apart the roots and stems, making sure that every division has both top growth and roots. If pieces can't be easily teased apart, use a sharp knife to separate equal sections. Pot up in fresh potting mix, making sure to plant them at the same depth as the original clump.

OFFSETS. Spider plants are among the most obliging producers of offsets for home propagation, sprouting endless "babies" at the ends of long, trailing stems. Bromeliads, cacti, and succulents form "pups," new plants that grow at the base of the parent plant. Separate pups from their parents when they are about one-third to one-half the size of the original plant, using a sharp knife to carefully cut them apart. Repot the parent plant and tuck the offset very lightly into a slight hole in moistened cactus potting mix. Use a stick in the pot to support the pup if needed; avoid sticking it too deeply into the medium. You can simply "pin" baby spider plants atop a container of moist potting soil, leaving them attached to their parent until they begin producing new leaves that signal their roots are growing too.

Check the plant profiles (beginning on page 46) for information about which houseplants are easily propagated and the best method to use for each.

♥ *INTRODUCING* ♥

BABY GREEN

BRIGHT
&
INDIRECT

1.95 LB

4 IN

DRY OUT
BETWEEN
WATERINGS

HIGH HUMIDITY
PREFERS 70-90°F

PART 2

INTRODUCING THE PLANTS
A to Z

African violets

(Saintpaulia hybrids)

A happy African violet will show off blooms year-round, in shades of pink, purple, magenta, or deep blue, as well as white and white-rimmed. Luckily for plant parents of all skill levels, these beauties with endearingly fuzzy foliage are among the easiest of the flowering houseplants to tend. Their petite size fits into any household. If your family includes fur babies, you can feel good about adopting an African violet too, as it poses no risk to a pet that nibbles at its leaves.

Date I brought you home: _____

What I loved about you from the start: _____

Milestones in your growth: _____

HELP ME GROW

► Bright, indirect or filtered light is best, although African violets tolerate lower (even artificial) light better than most blooming houseplants do.

WELLNESS CHECK: Brown spots are signs that your little one is getting too much direct sunlight. Pale foliage and spindly growth point to too little direct sunlight.

► Average to warm temperatures make African violets happiest. Dry air in your abode? Boost the humidity with a pebble tray (page 21). Or use a fine-mist spray bottle; just avoid cold water or large drops on the leaves.

► Your AV likes to be tucked into peaty and slightly acidic soil with good drainage. Repot every year or so with fresh soil for healthy growth—no need to move to a bigger pot. Trim your plant's roots by no more than one-third and settle them just a bit deeper in their remade bed.

FEED ME

► Keep the soil evenly moist but never soggy. Room-temperature water is just right, with no shock to the leaves. You can water from the bottom by setting your violet's pot in tepid water and letting it sip (no more than 30 minutes at a time). Self-watering pots can also be lifesavers for AV parents.

► Near-constant blooming can wear out your plant. Supply the nutrients it needs with a fertilizer designed for African violets, given every 2–3 weeks or as directed on the label.

LOVE ME

Good grooming: Pinch off spent flowers and use scissors to clip off lackluster leaves. If your AV gets dirty, avoid the temptation to bathe that fuzzy foliage—use a dry paintbrush to dust instead.

Enforce a strict bedtime: As much as they need bright light to grow, African violets also require at least 8 hours of darkness daily to keep blooming. Make sure yours is getting the nightly rest it needs, undisturbed by security lights shining in its window or round-the-clock lighting in an office setting.

More, please: Ready to expand your AV family? Use a sharp knife to cut off a leaf with an inch or two of stem, then plant it in fresh, pre-moistened soilless potting mix. Put the entire pot in a plastic bag and set it out of direct sunlight. Remove the bag and mist the cutting daily. Within a month, your cutting should develop roots, at which time you can remove it from the bag, but keep up with regular misting. In another month's time, expect to have a new baby to love.

Agaves

(Agave species)

While an adopted agave is unlikely to help you make your own tequila, these spiky-leaved succulents can bring a western desert vibe to your home's décor. Most agaves form a rosette of lancelike, fleshy foliage that may have toothed margins and sharp points at the tips. Some produce long, wavy leaves that may loll over the sides of their container, while others have more rigid, almost triangular foliage. To accommodate their prickly nature, choose a spot that permits looking without much risk of touching.

Date I brought you home: _____

What I loved about you from the start: _____

Milestones in your growth: _____

HELP ME GROW

▶ Naturally found in deserts, agaves prosper in bright light and will be happiest on a sunny windowsill where they get at least 5 hours of direct sun daily.

KEEP BABY SUN SAFE: While your agave can summer outdoors, make the move gradually. Even sun-loving agaves can suffer sunburn if abruptly relocated.

▶ Agaves can take the heat and will grow quite happily at normal to very warm household temperatures from spring through fall. During the winter, place your agave in a cooler location (50–55°F) for a bit of a rest.

▶ Nestle your agave's roots in a soil-based potting mix that has been amended with coarse sand or gravel for good drainage.

FEED ME

▶ Thoroughly moisten the potting soil when watering your agave but let the top two-thirds of the mix dry out before watering again. During the winter months when growth slows, water occasionally, just enough to prevent the potting soil from drying out completely.

DODGE SOGGY BOTTOMS: Avoid watering directly into your agave's leafy crown, make sure water drains away from the base of the plant after watering, and pour off water that drains into the saucer.

▶ Nourish your agave once a month with a serving of houseplant fertilizer from spring through the summer months. As lower light and cooler temperatures arrive in fall, cease feedings as baby slows down for a winter's rest.

LOVE ME

An old soul: Dubbed century plant, *Agave americana* was believed to bloom only once every one hundred years. In reality, this agave may bloom when it reaches age 10, but only plants growing outdoors are likely to produce flowers. Century plants grow slowly but their strappy leaves may reach 6 feet long as they age, so only young plants are suitable for indoor display. Varieties with creamy-yellow-striped leaves tend to grow the most slowly.

The agave queen: The most prized for growing indoors, Queen Victoria agave (*Agave victoriae-reginae*) produces dark green, geometrically spike-shaped, white-marked leaves in a rosette arrangement. Compact and slow-growing, this regal succulent would love to reign on your brightest windowsill.

Be supportive: Agaves' stiffly upright rosettes of fleshy leaves tend to outweigh their root systems, making them top-heavy and prone to tipping over. Secure your agave in a broad-based, heavy container to prevent spills.

Aloe

(Aloe barbadensis, a.k.a. Aloe vera)

Just like a grown child caring for a parent, some houseplants can care for you even as you care for them. The skin-soothing properties of the gel-like flesh inside an aloe plant's succulent leaves are well known. Cleopatra reportedly used aloe as part of her beauty regimen, and sunburn sufferers continue to seek its soothing relief. If cooling that sick burn isn't enough, aloe has another nifty trick to impress: it will reward your loving care with adorable grand-aloes, known as pups.

Date I brought you home: _____

What I loved about you from the start: _____

Milestones in your growth: _____

HELP ME GROW

▶ Your aloe will appreciate bright light, as from a south-facing window.

▶ Aloe is easygoing at most normal household temps and not finicky about humidity. Cooler conditions in winter, along with reduced watering and a pause in feedings, give it a healthy nap time.

▶ Well-drained, sandy to gritty soil-based potting mix is best for keeping aloe comfy in its pot. A layer of pebbles or coarse sand on top of the soil helps moisture drain away quickly from the base of the leaves and reduces the risk of rotting.

FEED ME

▶ Allow the top inch of soil in its pot to dry out between waterings. Aloe likes even moisture but a soggy situation makes it mopey and prone to rot. Cut back on watering in the winter.

▶ Nourish aloe monthly with houseplant fertilizer from spring into early fall. Give your aloe a break from fertilizing during the cooler months when its growth will slow down. Resume in the spring when light levels increase.

LOVE ME

More, please: If your aloe is happy, it will produce pups, baby plants or offsets, that arise from the base of the main plant. Use a sharp knife to separate the pups from the proud parent aloe and let the cut surfaces dry for a day or two before planting them in pots of their own.

Consistency is key: Easy-growing and long-lived, aloe will be your chlorophyll companion for many years if you meet its basic needs. While aloe prospers in bright light, direct sun can—ironically—give it a sunburn if you move it abruptly from indoors to an outside location. Likewise, relocating aloe into a lower light situation can turn it pale and sad.

Amaryllises

(Hippeastrum hortorum and hybrids)

These showy saucer-sized flowers are guaranteed to warm the heart of the proud plant parent who raises them from unremarkable-looking bulb to glorious bloom. Just a bit of parental love and care will help it produce a sturdy green stem topped by spectacular trumpet-shaped flowers in shades or combinations of red, pink, and white. Amaryllis bulbs bloom 6–8 weeks after they are planted. Long, strappy leaves accompany their upright flower stalks and persist through summer.

Date I brought you home: _____

What I loved about you from the start: _____

Milestones in your growth: _____

HELP ME GROW

▶ Bright light is essential for blooms. After its floral display is finished, the leafy bulb can spend the summer outdoors in a sunny spot; give it care and feeding to fuel next year's blossoms.

▶ Cool room temperatures (55–65°F) will support healthy growth and prolong flower life as you gently awaken your amaryllis from dormancy. Warmer temperatures will prompt buds to open more quickly but will also shorten flower life. After flowering, warmer temperatures (70–85°F) will keep your plant happy.

▶ To keep soggy conditions (and rot) away, use a soil-based potting mixture with roughly equal parts soil, perlite, and peat moss, and settle the bulb into its pot with the top third above soil level. Keep your amaryllis cozy and safe in a weighty pot that's no more than a couple of inches bigger in diameter than its bulb.

FEED ME

▶ Water your amaryllis thoroughly right after planting, and lightly thereafter, keeping the soil barely moist, until new growth begins to appear. Increase watering once things get growing but allow the top inch of potting mix to dry out between drinks. Maintain moisture throughout active growth, gradually weaning the bulb off water in late summer.

▶ Start feeding your amaryllis a balanced houseplant fertilizer when its new growth reaches 6 inches, serving it a helping every 10–14 days and continuing to supply nourishment into midsummer.

LOVE ME

Wake up, sleepyhead: Awaken your sleeping beauty by settling it into fresh potting soil and watering well. Keep it in cool conditions and water lightly as needed to keep the mix barely moist. When new growth appears and reaches 4–6 inches, move it into bright light. Increase watering and introduce a feeding schedule as described above.

Nap time is necessary: Getting your amaryllis to bloom in years to come requires you to help it into dormancy. Start cutting back on watering in mid- to late summer, gradually allowing the potting soil to dry out completely. Cut off the dried leaves and place the now-slumbering bulb in a cool (45–50°F), dark spot to nap for 10–12 weeks.

More, please: Well-raised amaryllis will produce small bulbs around the original bulb. Leave these youngsters attached to their mother bulb for one or two seasons before separating them.

Anthuriums

(Anthurium hybrids)

If you squint at the flowers of an anthurium, you can see how this showy tropical plant got the name "flamingo flower." Popular in floral arrangements, anthurium flowers may last for nearly 2 months, and a happy plant with adequate light may bloom almost year-round. These eye-catching conversation pieces will have your plant-parent heart bursting with pride.

Date I brought you home: _____

What I loved about you from the start: _____

Milestones in your growth: _____

HELP ME GROW

▶ Place your anthurium where it will enjoy bright but filtered, indirect light.

GET THE LIGHT RIGHT: Anthuriums will bloom in moderate light but direct sun can cause their leaf tips to brown. Keep your flower happy by giving it a spot within 3 feet of a window. In low lighting, anthuriums can grow pale and spindly.

▶ Tropical ancestry means anthuriums appreciate room temperatures around 65–80°F and humidity above what is usual in households. Place your anthurium's pot on top of a tray of pebbles and water for comfort.

▶ Peaty potting soil that is both moisture retentive and loose will keep your anthurium's roots feeling their best. A mix intended for African violets will also meet their needs. Keep roots cozy in a pot that's no more than an inch bigger in diameter than the plant's root- ball. Too much root space can discourage blooming.

FEED ME

▶ Water moderately so that your anthurium's potting mix stays evenly moist but not soggy. Let just the surface of the soil dry between waterings, but don't allow your darling to get too thirsty. In fall and winter, reduce watering enough to let the top half inch of the soil dry out before offering another drink.

▶ A fertilizer meant for flowering plants (containing more phosphorus than nitrogen) will help your anthurium produce its pretty flowers. Feed it once a month from spring through summer, then switch to a balanced food, applied every 1½–2 months, during fall and winter.

LOVE ME

Help me shine: Regularly wipe your anthurium's glossy dark green leaves with a damp cloth.

A special kind of flower: Each bloom is actually a group of flowers (an inflorescence) known as a spathe and spadix. The spathe, a modified leaf also called a bract, is the glossy and colorful, heart-shaped structure that surrounds the base of the spadix, the arching to twisty—depending on variety—stalk composed of many small flowers that rises from the center of the spathe. The flowers of the spadix can create a bit of a mess with their pollen; if neatness counts, you can snip off the floral protrusion and extend the display life of the glossy, waxy bract.

More, please: If your anthurium produces a new cluster of leaves arising from a separate growing point, divide your plant in early spring, making sure each piece has adequate roots and leaves. Tuck the new plant into its own pot and tend it with TLC. Anthuriums typically don't bloom until they are at least one year old.

Arrowhead plant
(Syngonium podophyllum)

For homes with limited light, an arrowhead plant can be a charming addition. You'll marvel at how its leaves change shape over time, from heart-shaped to more lobed and pointed. You can find syngoniums with prettily patterned or multicolored leaves to match your mood or décor. Your arrowhead plant will morph from bushy to vining as it ages, letting you shape its future by choosing to let it dangle from a basket or climb on a support.

Date I brought you home: _____

What I loved about you from the start: _____

Milestones in your growth: _____

HELP ME GROW

▶ Moderate light suits arrowhead plant just fine. Direct sunlight can make your baby uncomfortable and cause its leaves to turn pale and floppy. Give it a spot where it receives filtered or indirect light, like from a north- or east-facing window.

▶ Normal to warm room temperatures will keep your arrowhead plant happy and healthy. Average household humidity is okay too, although at warmer temperatures your precious will appreciate a bit of extra moisture in its air from a pebble tray or occasional misting.

▶ Arrowhead plants are easygoing and will gladly stretch their roots into any good-quality soil-based potting mixture. A modest-sized pot will meet its needs—even a mature arrowhead plant will be quite comfy in a 5- to 6-inch pot or vining from a 6- to 8-inch hanging basket.

FEED ME

▶ Maintain evenly, lightly moist soil for your arrowhead plant's comfort, but avoid overwatering or soggy conditions.

BABY NEEDS A REST. Back off on watering for a few weeks in the winter when lower light levels will cause growth to slow down. Give your plant a drink just often enough to keep the soil from drying completely during this time.

▶ Gently feed with a balanced houseplant fertilizer every 2 weeks during spring and summer; cut back to once per month during fall and winter.

LOVE ME

Hang out or help up: As your arrowhead plant begins to grow and vine, you can choose the display method that works best in your home. Let its stretching stems hang from above or give your growing arrowhead a structure to climb on and let it vine upward instead of dangling down. Help your arrowhead plant climb by gently tying or pinning its stems to the support you want it to climb on.

More, please: Arrowhead plant's fleshy stems feature knobby nodes and are sheathed in papery brown. Aerial roots tend to occur naturally at the nodes, making it easy to create more little plants. Just snip off a stem below one of those rooty nodes and peel away the lowest leaf and papery sheath. Tuck the cut end into a pot of moistened potting soil and cover the pot with a plastic bag to keep things moist and humid. Place in bright to moderate, indirect light and monitor to make sure things don't dry out. Rooting should happen within 1–2 months, after which you can remove the cover and water normally. Begin fertilizing a month after that; within 6 months you can treat your grand-plants just like their parent.

Asparagus ferns

(Asparagus setaceus, Asparagus densiflorus, and varieties)

No Hollandaise sauce needed to enjoy the delicate foliage of these close relatives of the vegetable of the same name. While their texture is fernlike, the non-garden types of asparagus are ferns in name only. What appear to be fronds are actually green stems covered in modified branchlets, called cladophylls. Whether your family plan includes the ethereal asparagus fern or one of the more upright and plumy emerald or foxtail ferns, these friends offer a nice visual contrast to houseplants like dieffenbachia or fiddle-leaf fig that have broad, thick leaves.

Date I brought you home: _____

What I loved about you from the start: _____

Milestones in your growth: _____

HELP ME GROW

▶ Your little 'gus will appreciate bright, indirect light; too much sun can cause yellowing or browning of leaves.

▶ Average to cool room temperatures keep asparagus fern happy. At warmer temperatures, especially when the heat is on, your baby will appreciate increased humidity to keep it from shedding its tiny branchlets.

SEND TO SUMMER CAMP? Your asparagus fern may look dainty but it can tolerate a summer outdoors, as long as you keep it sheltered out of direct sunshine.

▶ Fill your asparagus fern's pot with a good-quality soil-based potting mix and leave room between the soil and the rim of the container for the fleshy roots that tend to grow close to the surface. Repot when the roots begin to crowd the sides of the pot, moving up a container size every year or two.

FEED ME

▶ Water with the goal of keeping the potting mixture evenly moist without letting your asparagus fern sit in soggy conditions. Cut back on the drinks in winter, but avoid letting the soil dry out completely or your baby will drop its feathery foliage in a hot minute.

▶ Serve up a balanced liquid fertilizer every 2–3 weeks throughout the spring and summer months, then reduce feedings to once per month in fall and winter to help baby rest.

LOVE ME

This one's a gem: Emerald fern (*Asparagus densiflorus* 'Sprengeri'), also called Sprenger's fern, is a deeper green and sturdier looking than the asparagus fern, although its bolder foliage consists of the same modified branch structures. It will enjoy the same conditions as asparagus fern.

Hey, mister! When the heat comes on in your house, break out the spray bottle to keep your asparagus fern comfy. Make sure it's not sitting in the path of a heating vent, and spritz occasionally or group with other plants on a pebble tray to make the air around it adequately moist. This fondness for a bit of humidity makes asparagus fern a good candidate for keeping you company in the bathroom, where you can sing to it while you shower.

A foxy friend: Foxtail fern (*Asparagus densiflorus* 'Myersii'), a.k.a. Myers fern, produces an upright cluster of bottlebrush-like, bright green stems that may reach 2 feet tall. Treat it as described for asparagus fern.

Baby's tears
(Soleirolia soleirolii)

While it may sound like something to be avoided at all costs, baby's tears produces such enchanting cascades of adorable tiny leaves as to make its plant parent practically weep with joy. The delicate, nubbly texture of baby's tears makes an attractive contrast with bold, architectural plants such as rubber plant, sansevieria, or palms. Display it on its own in a smooth, modern container that's tall enough to allow baby's "tresses" to dangle over the sides. A hanging basket that allows baby's tears to sprawl pleasingly over its edges also makes a pretty setting for this charming plant.

Date I brought you home: _____

What I loved about you from the start: _____

Milestones in your growth: _____

HELP ME GROW

▶ Baby's tears appreciates moderate to bright, indirect light. Full sun can cause brownish scorching of its tiny leaves.

▶ Cool room temperatures suit baby's tears best. The warmer baby's tears' environment is, the more it will cry for humid air around its foliage. This is a good plant to house in your bathroom, where it will enjoy the steamy conditions. Elsewhere in the house, a pebble tray under its pot can help to supply additional moisture.

▶ Richly organic potting soil will help to keep your baby's tears happy. Repot into a larger container in late spring when the plant has filled its pot and its roots are becoming crowded.

ROOM TO GROW: If it seems like your little darling is constantly thirsting for more water, it's time for a bigger pot.

FEED ME

▶ Maintain evenly moist soil throughout spring, summer, and fall when baby's tears is vigorously growing, then cut back on watering in the winter. Don't let the potting soil dry out completely, or baby's tears will become wilty and brown.

▶ Baby's tears tends to grow without too much prompting. A monthly feeding with a dilute liquid houseplant fertilizer will meet its needs without overfeeding.

LOVE ME

Deceivingly dainty: Petite foliage and fine-textured stems that never reach more than 4 inches tall may make baby's tears seem delicate. But a happy baby is a vigorous grower that can quickly overtake companions in a shared container. Its diminutive size and love of humidity make it a good choice for a terrarium.

A little off the top: Practice your tonsorial skills and keep baby's tears looking trim and tidy with the occasional snip of the scissors. Snipping off stem tips promotes bushy, compact growth and is a way to remove brown leaves caused by dry air, dry soil, or sunburn. But long stems with few leaves may indicate that the temperature is too warm for baby's tears, and constant wilting or browning indicates that baby's tears is not happy. If you're often trimming in response to these problems, get to the root of the situation and move baby's tears to a place where it is more comfortable.

More, please: When it's time to repot an overcrowded baby's tears, you can separate yours into more plants by gently dividing the mass of leafy stems and wiry roots into two or more clumps. Repot each in fresh soil and give extra TLC—especially humidity—for a few weeks until the divisions are settled in their new containers.

Banana plants

(Musa species and varieties)

Cartoons may have taught you that bananas grow on trees, but banana plants actually are evergreen perennials. It's safest to select a dwarf variety for growing indoors—even these may reach heights of 6 feet. Be prepared to love your banana plant for what it is, not for what it might give you to eat. Not all species or varieties of banana yield edible fruits, and even those that do are unlikely to produce flowers or fruits when growing indoors. It's a dramatic accent plant that is safe for all pets.

Date I brought you home: _____

What I loved about you from the start: _____

Milestones in your growth: _____

HELP ME GROW

▶ Bright light and plenty of it help your baby banana thrive. Still, young leaves may scorch in direct sun, especially if its soil or the air around it is too dry.

▶ Warmer than average indoor temperatures keep banana plants cozy, along with humid conditions that you can create by misting the broad leaves occasionally.

NOT COOL. In Florida and other near-tropical locations, bananas may grow outdoors year-round, and in temperate regions it's possible to let them spend the summer months outside. But the slightest hint of a chill (50°F or lower) can send your banana plant into decline.

▶ Give your banana plant an ample and sturdy container filled with rich, soil-based potting mix. Good drainage is important to avoid rotting. Repot young plants into bigger containers as often as needed. Mature plants will benefit from repotting to refresh their soil every year or two.

FEED ME

▶ Banana's big leaves let it lose lots of water, so it needs regular drinks. Maintain even moisture but let the top of the potting soil dry out slightly between waterings. Cut back on the drinks during winter when lower light will cause growth to slow, but watch your banana baby closely for browning leaves or other signs of moisture stress caused by dry indoor air.

▶ Bananas grow rapidly during the spring and summer months and need a nourishing diet to support healthy growth of their substantial foliage. Provide liquid fertilizer every 2–3 weeks from spring through fall, then cut back to monthly feeding during the winter.

LOVE ME

Roll with it: Your banana will grow to be a big, bold, beautiful member of your household. To make sure you are able to move your baby when you rearrange furniture, clean nearby, or turn the plant for even light exposure, put it on a wheeled saucer or platform.

Show leaves some love: Consider traffic patterns when choosing a spot for your banana's home base. Those huge leaves are rather delicate and can tear easily if they're regularly jostled. Keep this in mind if baby goes out for the summer—place it in a spot protected from winds. Wherever your banana hangs out, wipe leaves with a damp cloth to remove dust and debris.

More, please: Banana "pups" will arise from the base of mature, happy plants and can be separated from the main plant in early spring.

Begonias

(Begonia species, hybrids and cultivars)

Although there are begonias grown for their outstanding blooms, the most popular houseplant choices are those with fantastically spotted, swirled, or multicolored foliage. Leaves with dramatically marked veins, fringed edges, bumpy surfaces, or even a metallic finish may be what attracted you to your own special begonia, but pretty pink or white flowers that appear throughout the year could further endear you to the plant.

Date I brought you home: _____

What I loved about you from the start: _____

Milestones in your growth: _____

HELP ME GROW

▶ Moderate to bright, indirect or filtered light will satisfy the needs of your begonia. Direct sun can damage its leaves.

BRIGHTER FOR BLOOMING: If your begonia is meant for showy flowers rather than fancy foliage, it will appreciate more light than its leafy kin. Place your bloomer to receive 3–4 hours of direct sunlight each day.

▶ Your begonia will be comfy at normal household temperatures; just protect it from temperatures above 80°F or below 55°F. Pay attention to humidity, especially during winter. Provide a pebble tray or use a mister but avoid wetting the leaves.

▶ Light and loose soilless potting mix that contains peat and perlite puts begonia roots at ease and reduces the risk of rotting. Match the container to your begonia's root type: Fibrous-rooted types such as angel-wing begonias can be kept in a pot that's slightly snug and repotted in spring. Begonias growing from rhizomes prefer a broader, shallower container. All require excellent drainage.

FEED ME

▶ Keep your begonia's soil moist but avoid soggy conditions. Watering from the bottom helps. Reduce watering in winter but never let the potting mix dry out completely.

▶ Serve your begonia baby a balanced houseplant fertilizer every 2–3 weeks from spring through fall. Encourage a bloomer with food that has higher phosphorus, such as a formulation for African violets.

LOVE ME

Angel wings and begonia kings: Wing-shaped leaves and dangling flower clusters are the enchanting features of angel-wing begonias, favorites for their ease of care. Rex begonias (*Begonia rex*), a.k.a. painted-leaf begonias, and other species grown for their fancy foliage tend to be more finicky.

Be supportive: Angel-wing begonias carry their showy leaves on jointed, succulent stems that can be rather floppy. Displaying your not-so-little angel-wing in a hanging pot is one way to appreciate its relaxed nature, or you can tuck a few discreet supports in among the leaves.

More, please: A nifty way to replicate your favorite foliage-forward begonia is by cutting a section of leaf with a few veins and sticking it into moist seed-starting medium so the veins are in contact with the soil. Mist and then cover with a plastic bag and place in a warm spot out of direct sunlight. Within 1½–2 months, roots and leaves should form. A somewhat speedier method is to follow the leaf-cutting method used for African violets (see page 49).

Bonsai

Few houseplants are more captivating than a bonsai, a term that describes the traditional Japanese art form of training plants rather than a single kind of plant. Bonsai involves pruning and training plants to create specimens that resemble mature trees in miniature. Although evergreen and deciduous trees are popular bonsai subjects, skilled bonsai practitioners can shape almost any plant into a bonsai. Among the most common plants grown as bonsai are juniper, Chinese elm, ficus, azalea, jade plant, and umbrella tree. How you care for your own bonsai baby depends to a large extent upon what kind of plant it is.

Date I brought you home: _____

What I loved about you from the start: _____

Milestones in your growth: _____

HELP ME GROW

▶ Bright light, including 3–4 hours of direct sun daily, is necessary if your bonsai is a tree that would normally grow large in a temperate landscape instead of on a windowsill. Bonsai formed from plants normally grown as houseplants will have the same light requirements as their non-bonsai kin.

MAYBE USE A FILTER: Bonsai plants spending the summer outdoors may need sun protection. Place your bonsai where it gets its daily rays in the morning or late afternoon, or through filtering leaves.

▶ From spring into early fall, your bonsai will be happy in normal to cool household temperatures (60–70°F). If it will be summering outdoors, move it outside when nighttime temperatures reliably exceed 40°F. During the winter, place your bonsai in cool conditions (50–60°F) and keep it away from dry air. Humidity is important to keeping a bonsai comfy, too. Mist your baby regularly when it's actively growing. Place it on a pebble tray in winter and mist occasionally.

▶ Special bonsai soil consisting of granular clay particles provides both the drainage and moisture retention that a bonsai requires. Depending on your species, its pot may contain a mix that includes these hard clay granules along with coarse sand and compost or peat moss. Repot in spring when you notice the pot becoming crowded. Reduce the roots by one-third when repotting and replant in fresh growing medium.

FEED ME

▶ Your bonsai's reduced root system makes it all the more dependent on you for its water needs. Take care that your bonsai never dries out while also avoiding standing water around the roots. Water thoroughly until liquid runs out of the pot's drainage holes, then allow the excess to drain. You can also submerge the pot for no more than 30 minutes to water it and to flush away excess salts from fertilizers. Reduce watering in the winter but do not let the soil dry out entirely.

▶ Feed your bonsai with houseplant fertilizer or bonsai food every 4–6 weeks throughout the growing season. Stop fertilizing during the winter when your bonsai may be dormant or in slow growth.

LOVE ME

Parenting support: To learn more about this ancient art, seek out the company of other bonsai practitioners and aficionados. Check social media for a bonsai group near you. The American Bonsai Society (absbonsai.org) can provide support and guidance (and sources of more beautifully shaped plants).

Boston fern

(Nephrolepis exaltata)

Bringing a Boston fern into your home is a lot like adopting a large, shaggy dog, absent the barking. Your new family member is an exuberant and substantial presence that will bask in your attention and tend to shed all over your house. Its bright green fronds may stretch to 12–20 inches long and a happy Boston fern may grow 2–3 feet tall and wide. Place your BF in a hanging basket or atop a pedestal, where its leafy limbs can stretch out all around it like a green ferny fountain.

Date I brought you home: _____

What I loved about you from the start: _____

Milestones in your growth: _____

HELP ME GROW

▶ Boston ferns are popular poolside and patio décor, where they will appreciate a spot sheltered from direct sun. Give your BF bright light but shield it from harsh rays that can scorch its foliage. Indoors, it will do well near a south or east window.

▶ Normal to slightly cool room temperatures (50–70°F) will keep your Boston fern feeling fine. As the temperature climbs, so will your fern's need for humidity. Spritz your BF every few days in hot weather or in winter when heating makes the air in your home too dry for your baby's comfort.

▶ Your Boston fern's roots will feel right at home in a peat-based potting mix. When the roots begin to crowd its pot, move your BF to a larger size in spring, refreshing the potting soil at the same time.

FEED ME

▶ Don't let your fern get thirsty. Keep its soil evenly moist and it will grow happily in your care. If your BF spends the winter in a cool space (50–55°F), let the top of the potting mix dry out between waterings.

▶ From spring through fall, give your Boston fern a feeding with houseplant fertilizer every 2–4 weeks.

LOVE ME

Cries for help: Several things can cause your Boston fern's fronds to go from pretty green to pale to crispy brown. Dry air, dry soil, too much sun, too-warm temperatures, or lack of nutrients all may make your BF sad and weepy (i.e., dropping leaflets everywhere). Your baby will lose some leaves naturally as it ages, but overall browning of leaf tips indicates that something is amiss. Check moisture first, and use scissors to snip off browning tips and faded fronds.

One good fern turn: If your BF sits near a bright window, make sure to give its pot a quarter turn every so often to prevent it from growing unevenly in the direction of the light.

More, please: If your Boston fern is happy and well adjusted, it will produce new young plants around the outer edges of the original. You can separate these from the parent plant in spring and give them their own pots to spread out in.

Bromeliads

(Bromeliaceae)

Dramatic, arching, and sometimes spine-rimmed leaves and showy, long-lasting flowers make bromeliads stand out among houseplants. The bromeliad family (Bromeliaceae), sometimes referred to as the pineapple family for its famous member, includes numerous species of epiphytic and terrestrial plants, many of which form spiral-shaped rosettes of stiff foliage surrounding a central cup for catching rainwater. The epiphytes in the family are tree dwellers in their natural state and reliant on capturing moisture and nutrients with their leaves rather than taking them up with their roots, which are wiry and serve mainly as anchors. Terrestrial bromeliads have more use for soil than their aerial kin but also catch water from above.

Date I brought you home: _____

What I loved about you from the start: _____

Milestones in your growth: _____

HELP ME GROW

▶ Light needs among bromeliads vary by species. Some will do best in bright but filtered or indirect light, while others need daily direct sun exposure. As a general rule, epiphytic species prefer bright, filtered light and terrestrial bromeliads appreciate some direct sunlight.

HEIGHT DICTATES LIGHT: In their native rainforest conditions, each tree-dwelling epiphytic bromeliad species has its preferred location. Those that live on tree trunks down below the canopy typically have soft, flexible leaves, while those that inhabit branches closer to the tops of trees often have stiff, leathery foliage. Use this as a clue to what your own bromeliad will like in lighting: if its leaves are thin and soft, provide filtered light; thicker and rigid leaves indicate a need for brighter conditions and even a bit of direct sun.

▶ Tropical and subtropical origins mean that bromeliads enjoy normal to warm household temperatures all year round and appreciate high humidity. Prolonged exposure to temperatures below 55°F can cause injury to bromeliads' leaves.

▶ Good drainage and ample aeration are the keys to supporting a bromeliad's roots. Potting mixes sold for orchids will serve your bromeliad's needs; look for a mix that combines peat moss or coir (coconut fiber) and leaf mold or potting soil in equal parts. Depending on the species you've adopted, it may need only a shallow pot or even a suitable porous surface such as a branch to be mounted upon rather than planted in.

SUPPORT CAN BE BEAUTIFUL: Epiphytic bromeliads may grow quite happily when displayed on a branch or moss-stuffed wire form. With their slender roots wrapped in moistened sphagnum moss, you can secure your bromeliads to a likely log or piece of cork bark with florist's wire to create a colorful and exotic display.

FEED ME

▶ Water your bromeliad with filtered or distilled water or with rainwater. Bromeliads are sensitive to chemicals in softened water, while hard water will leave deposits on the foliage. Maintain water constantly in the central cup of your bromeliad, turning the plant over once a month to empty the reservoir of old water, then sprinkling the leaves and refilling the cup with a fresh drink. Moisten the potting soil of terrestrial types when the top half inch becomes dry. Mist air plants or soak them every few days.

▶ Serve a dilute liquid fertilizer in modest amounts, based on your bromeliad's specific requirements.

LOVE ME ♥

BLUSHING BROMELIAD (*NEOREGELIA CAROLINAE* 'TRICOLOR')

Flashy foliage: You won't feel shy about showing off this pretty plant that delivers long-lasting color with its rosette of yellow- and green-striped leaves that blush bright red around the central cup as the plant begins to bloom. While the flowers remain tucked inside the cup, the blushing leaves put on a show for some months.

Fill my cup: Moisten the potting mix regularly and keep the central cup filled, refreshing the water every 2 weeks. Once a month give your blushing bromeliad half-strength fertilizer meant for flowering plants (more phosphorus than nitrogen). Go easy on the feedings—too much will diminish the colors of the leaves.

More, please: Gradually the parent plant dies back after its colorful foliar display, making way for "pups" that can be separated and planted in peat-based potting mix in pots of their own. Give newly planted offsets humid conditions to help them get settled. Humidity, bright light, and warm temperatures will keep them feeling at home.

URN PLANT, SILVER VASE PLANT (*AECHMEA FASCIATA*)

Lovely, leathery leaves: The broad, arching, and waxy foliage of the urn plant appears brushed and banded with silver. The handsome leaves form an upright vase that surrounds a central cup for catching water. Refresh that water every couple of weeks; mist and rinse the leaves when watering, and keep your urn plant's potting soil evenly moist.

One and done: Urn plants bloom when they reach maturity—around 3–4 years, producing a long-lasting flower spike composed of showy pink bracts and small purple flowers. Provide bright light to encourage blooming, and fertilize every month in spring and summer with a dilute liquid fertilizer for flowering plants.

More, please: After it blooms, your urn plant will begin to die back, but it won't leave you sad and alone in its wake. Two to three offsets normally form around the base of the waning parent plant, providing you with new urn plants to raise and love. Pot these up in a mix of potting soil and peat moss and care for them as you did their parent.

Bulbs, corms, and tubers

Bringing home a bouncing baby "bulb" can fill your home with amazing fragrance, beautiful blooms, or dramatic foliage. Bright tulips or a regal Easter lily may bring you cheer for a few weeks in favorable conditions. Once the flowers fade, though, the show is over. Bulbs that have been "forced"—grown intentionally to bloom indoors—typically lack the resources to live on and bloom again in another year's time. While it's not impossible to coax forced bulbs to repeat their performance, even with specialized care it may not be successful. The casual plant parent may choose to let this relationship fade to make room on the windowsill for a more enduring, if perhaps less glamorous, adoptee.

Date I brought you home: _____

What I loved about you from the start: _____

Milestones in your growth: _____

You are a: _____

HELP ME GROW

▶ Bright light helps bulbs, corms, and tubers awaken from dormancy.

GUIDE MY GROWTH: Turn the container every few days as your bulbs' shoots develop to keep them from bending toward the light.

▶ Bulbs that move outdoors after blooming will enjoy bright but filtered light while their leaves do the work of stockpiling food for next year's display. Avoid moving abruptly from household lighting to direct sun.

▶ Cool temperatures help keep bulbs' foliage and flower stalks sturdy and stocky as they wake up and prepare to bloom. Once they start blooming, warm household temperatures will prompt buds to open rapidly, while cool conditions will make the flowers last longer.

PLAY IT COOL: If your warm house is causing bulbs to hit the flowering gas, try moving them into a cool room at night to prolong their good looks.

▶ While soil needs vary, most bulbs, corms, and tubers need good drainage to prevent their fleshy storage structure from rotting. Well-drained potting soil amended with coarse sand is best for most; some, such as paperwhites and hyacinths, will bloom happily with their roots resting in a bed of pebbles and water.

FEED ME

▶ Even moisture during active growth is necessary for most bulbs and other rooty plant babies. Water regularly to keep things modestly moist but never soggy.

▶ Feeding is unnecessary if your bulby bloomers will only stay for a single show. If you plan to plant them outdoors after their flowers fade, give them a bit of liquid fertilizer when you water; this will help prolong the flowers as well. Specific fertilizer needs follow.

LOVE ME

CALADIUM, ELEPHANT'S EARS (*CALADIUM* HYBRIDS)

Who needs flowers? The showy, colorful leaves that arise from caladium's tender tubers are enough to make you forget about flowers. Broad, heart-shaped foliage in shades of red, pink, green, white, and cream, often with contrasting veins and matching colorful stems, reaches 12–15 inches long and puts on a lovely leafy display for several months in the summer.

Comfy in the heat: Your pretty angel wings—another common name for caladium—is true to its tropical origins and will not tolerate even the slightest hint of a chill. In your house it will enjoy a spot with bright light and high humidity that can be difficult to maintain. Caladium is popular for outdoor containers in shady to filtered light. Its handsome leaves are paper-thin and need constant moisture to keep them looking their best.

Napping happy: From late spring into fall, caladiums will create a tropical effect with their glamorous foliage. But when the days turn cool, it's necessary nap time for your leafy darlings. Grow these tender tubers in peaty potting soil and keep them where they are protected from drafts and cold air. Feed them weekly with fertilizer that features nitrogen to boost their foliage and help them build reserves for their rest period. You can discard them when cold winds blow, or let the pots dry out as fall arrives. Snip off dead leaves and stems and set the containers in a dark spot where temperatures won't fall below 55°F. In spring, repot the tubers in fresh potting mix.

CALLA LILIES (*ZANTEDESCHIA* HYBRIDS)

Spring bloomer: Arising from rhizomes to dazzle with their elegant and colorful blooms, lovely calla lilies are not lilies at all. But pots of these blooming beauties often keep company in the spring with true lilies sold for Easter, and their pink, yellow, red, cream, or bicolored floral cups pair nicely with Easter lilies' white trumpets.

Cut your losses: Snip off flower stalks as the blooms fade and continue to care for your calla's arrow- to lance-shaped leaves until late summer. Keep the potting soil evenly moist and feed monthly with a houseplant fertilizer for flowering plants while your calla is actively growing. If you're not inclined to take the steps necessary to give calla lily rhizomes a dry nap late in the summer, or if your calla is producing fewer, smaller flowers after a few years of display, it might be time to let it go and plan for a new pot of callas in spring.

Summer sleeper: Your calla will want to nap in late summer. Cut way back on watering and let the leaves dry up; cut off old foliage and place the pot in a cool, dim spot. Water just enough to keep the potting soil from drying out completely. Repot rhizomes in late fall before placing them in a warm, bright location and watering to awaken them.

DAFFODILS, PAPERWHITES (*NARCISSUS* CULTIVARS)

Poetry in a pot: Out in the garden, daffodils are among the earliest flowers to awaken, sometimes poking their cheery cup-and-saucer heads up through a blanket of snow. Indoors, your own pot of perfect golden daffo-darlings can brighten the dark days of late winter and remind you that spring is on its way.

Scents and sensibility: Paperwhite narcissus deliver lovely fragrance from their bountiful white flowers. Paperwhite bulbs don't need to be chilled during dormancy like other daffodils do, and they will begin growing as soon as you supply them with warmth, light, and moisture. You can even grow paperwhites without soil by resting the base of the bulb in pebbles with water up around the roots. Pay close attention to the water level and don't let your paperwhites dry out. Other daffodils may be potted up in fall and placed in a refrigerator or unheated garage for the 3–4 months of chilling they need to get ready to bloom. Compact varieties are best for indoor enjoyment, whether you force your own or buy a pot on the brink of blooming. Keep your daffodils in a bright but cool location to prolong the life of their flowers and to keep the foliage from growing stretched and pale. Weekly applications of liquid houseplant food will promote floral life and healthy green leaves.

Afterblooms: Once paperwhites have finished blooming, their life as attractive houseplants is pretty well over. Toss them out and turn your attention to other sprouts in your life. Other potted daffodils may be moved to outdoor living after their indoor display has faded. Keep watering and feeding until their leaves fade; repot or plant in the ground in fall.

EASTER LILY (*LILIUM LONGIFLORUM*)

Heralds of spring: Looking as though they are poised to trumpet the arrival of spring, Easter lilies carry their substantial white flowers atop tall stems covered in lance-shaped leaves. When shopping for a pot of these lovelies, choose a plant with many buds and few, if any, fully opened flowers. Give it a spot in bright light, and water to keep the potting mix lightly moist. Cool temperatures will keep your Easter lily happy and extend the life of its pretty flowers. Placing the pot in a cool (65°F) room at night will help, even if it spends its days in warmer conditions. Feed your lily with liquid houseplant fertilizer every 2–3 weeks if you want to plant it out in the garden after its time in your home.

Ditch the wrapper: If you bring your lovely lily home with a wrapper of bright foil or (now more common) colorful plastic around its pot, remove the covering to prevent a slow death by drowning due to impaired drainage. A soggy bottom is no good for your lily, even in the short few weeks it may spend in your life. If you don't like the look of its unadorned plastic pot, slip it into a larger, more attractive outer (cache) pot, but make sure it doesn't sit in water.

Pollen prevention: The bright golden yellow pollen borne in the middle of each pristine white blossom can create unwelcome messes on surfaces below. Snip out the pollen-bearing anthers from fully opened flowers to prolong flower life and avoid yellow stains on your furniture.

FREESIA (*FREESIA CORYMBOSA*)

Sweetly scented: From insignificant-looking corms, freesias produce curving stalks of open cup-shaped flowers that emit a lovely fragrance. Natives of South Africa, freesia corms need a 2-month period of warm conditioning in late summer (versus the chilling required by other bulbs) before they are potted up and moved into average room-temperature conditions to begin growing. Plant them in well-drained potting soil and keep them lightly moist during their active growth period, feeding them every 2 weeks with liquid fertilizer for flowering plants. A cool, bright window is their preferred location for bud formation and blooming. Continue to care for them after the flowers have faded and until the foliage dies back, then let the pots dry out and store the corms in cool, dark, dry conditions.

Be supportive: Freesias produce their fragrant flowers on stems that may stretch 12–18 inches tall. Growing indoors, these flower stalks may tend toward floppy behavior and need a bit of parental support to help them hold their heads high.

GRAPE HYACINTHS (*MUSCARI* SPECIES)

Adorably easy: Petite grape hyacinth bulbs grow into the most adorable little plants, with strappy grasslike leaves and clusters of sweet-scented purple, blue, or white flowers that look like loose clusters of tiny grapes. Grape hyacinths are easy to force for bloom indoors and make attractive companions for other spring bulbs both indoors and out.

Free-range flower friends: Feed your grape hyacinths every 2 weeks with a liquid houseplant fertilizer while they are actively growing and until their foliage fades after they've finished flowering. If you love them, you can continue to care for them and repeat the forcing process. Or you can plant them outdoors. Small bulbs like grape hyacinths are popular choices for naturalizing—planting them in loose groupings in a lawn, for example. They will grow and increase in such conditions for years to come.

HYACINTHS (*HYACINTHUS ORIENTALIS* HYBRIDS)

Heady aroma: The fragrance of a hyacinth in full bloom is amazing and pervasive. These stiffly upright spikes covered in starry florets of pink, purple, blue, white, yellow, or orange are beloved by many for their signature scent. Be careful if you're bringing your hyacinth home to live in close quarters; the aroma can be overpowering in unventilated small spaces. Cool temperatures indoors will help extend the life of your hyacinth's flowers, but even so, each flower spike will last for no more than a couple weeks.

Forced for good: You can buy hyacinth bulbs in fall and pot them up for forcing by exposing them to 3 months of cold temperatures before bringing them into light and warmth to bloom. Like paperwhite narcissus, hyacinths may be brought into bloom in a bed of pebbles and water or in a specialized bulb vase that supports the bulb so just its roots are in the water. Forced hyacinths tend not to recover from this experience however, and you should plan to discard the bulbs once their flowering is completed. If you can't bear to toss them out, hyacinths may be moved outdoors and their bulbs planted in the garden in fall. They may return to bloom after a few seasons.

TULIPS (*TULIPA* SPECIES AND HYBRIDS)

Tulip mania: The pleasure of a pot of blooming tulips offers just a glimpse into the craze that swept the Netherlands in the 17th century. Like other bulbs discussed here, tulips can be forced for indoor flowering by providing them with a 3- to 4-month chilling period before they are brought into warm, bright conditions and awakened from their dormancy. You can force any kind of tulip that catches your eye, but the best choices for this treatment are the smaller species and cultivars. Types that are naturally tall and/or with hefty double flowers are prone to toppling and flopping when grown indoors.

A passing fancy: Whether you buy a pot of tulips primed and ready to bloom or force your own, you'll want to enjoy the rather brief time you have with these beautiful and often sweet-scented flowers. At most, their indoor display will last for a couple of weeks. The best you can do is encourage long flower life by keeping their soil lightly moistened, feeding them a bit of liquid fertilizer with their water, and providing cool growing conditions. Warm temperatures, especially, will hasten tulips' decline and prompt the cup-shaped flowers to open wide until the petals lay almost flat. If your warm home is making your tulips hurry along, try setting them in a cool room overnight and enjoying their company in your living space during the daytime.

Tulip afterlife: Once they've been forced, tulips' prospects for repeating their life cycle are only so-so. Too much energy goes into forming those glorious blooms, and the bulbs don't often recover. Species that produce smaller plants and flowers stand a somewhat better chance of living on if you plant them out in your garden following their stint indoors.

Cacti

With spines to protect them and moisture-storing capacity, cacti are remarkably self-sufficient. This is not to suggest that your prickly little adoptee doesn't need tending. You may lavish affection on a mammillaria just as you would an African violet, but with dramatically different watering practices. The cacti described here represent some of the desert cactus species most commonly grown as houseplants. Schlumbergeras (Christmas cactus and kin, profiled separately) are jungle or forest cacti and have different care requirements.

Date I brought you home: _____

What I loved about you from the start: _____

Milestones in your growth: _____

You are a: _____

HELP ME GROW

▶ Cacti need bright, full sunlight year-round. Give yours a spot in the sunniest window in your home and, if possible, let cacti spend the summer months outdoors in a sunny spot.

EVEN THINGS OUT: Promote well-rounded development by turning the pot about a quarter turn twice a week.

AVOID ABRUPT CHANGES: Make moves gradually, going from indoors to a shady outdoor spot and then to partial sun over a period of a few weeks. Reverse this process when it's time for cacti to move back indoors, making sure to start it before the weather turns cold.

▶ Average to warm household temperatures are just right for cacti during the spring and summer when plants are actively growing. In fall and winter, your cactus needs a rest and will be happiest with bright light and cool nighttime temperatures (50–60°F). This cool rest period is especially important if you want your cactus to bloom.

▶ Excellent drainage is the main requirement of any potting mixture for growing cacti. Mixtures designed for cacti are widely available or you can blend your own using potting soil well amended with coarse sand and/or perlite. Refresh the potting soil in spring and move to a larger pot as needed.

▶ **HANDLE WITH CARE:** Repotting can pose risks for you and your prickly sprout. Wear gloves and use tongs or layered newspaper to gently grasp your cactus as you lift it from its pot. Take care to repot it at the same depth, holding it at the proper level and scooping or pouring lightly moistened potting mix around its roots to fill the container. Avoid firming the soil around the roots, and don't water immediately after repotting.

FEED ME

▶ During the spring and summer when your cactus is actively growing, water lightly but frequently, allowing the top half inch to inch of the mix to dry out in between. Or you can set the pot in room-temperature water just long enough to allow the mix to become saturated, then remove it from the water and let the excess drain off. If watering from above, apply water to the soil rather than the plant and avoid letting water puddle on or around your cactus. In any season, underwatering is preferable to overwatering for cacti.

SLOW THE WATER IN WINTER: A cactus that is resting in cool conditions in the winter will need very little water. Check occasionally for shriveling; water in the morning when necessary and use a light touch. If your cactus seems thirsty, water lightly over a few days rather than heavily all at once.

▶ Your cactus needs light nourishment in spring and summer and nothing to eat during its winter rest period. Serve it cactus-specific fertilizer according to the label instructions.

LOVE ME ♥

BALL CACTI (*PARODIA* SPECIES)

Have a ball: Globe-shaped when young, some species of ball cacti grow into columnar shapes as they age, producing offsets around their base. Clusters of ½- to ¾-inch spines cover ball cactus in attractive symmetrical arrangements, giving them a fuzzy appearance; spines may be light-colored or golden yellow, earning these adorable cacti names like silver ball and golden ball.

Pleasingly petite: Mature ball cacti may stretch into columns of 12–18 inches, but most remain rounded and no more than 10 inches tall. Different species bloom in summer in shades of yellow, orange, or red.

PERUVIAN APPLE CACTUS (*CEREUS REPANDUS*, A.K.A. *CEREUS PERUVIANUS*)

Classic good looks: Producing a gray-green column with pronounced, spine-covered ridges, this cactus makes a handsome upright accent amid pots of rounded, low-growing plants. Peruvian apple cactus may grow to 3 feet tall, but keeping it in a 4-inch-diameter pot will keep it to a more manageable size.

Renowned night bloomer: If you let your cereus mature to its full height, it may reward you with fragrant flowers in summer. This cactus's white, 6-inch-long, funnel-shaped flowers open at night and fade by morning.

Be supportive: Choose a heavy container for your Peruvian apple cactus to balance the weight of its tall, sturdy column and reduce the risk of tipping over. Wear gloves and enlist help when moving it outdoors for the summer or back in for the winter, and place it in spots where it is unlikely to be bumped or knocked over by strong winds.

PINCUSHION CACTUS, POWDER PUFF CACTUS (*MAMMILLARIA* SPECIES)

Nubby and nice: Globe-shaped to columnar, cacti in the genus *Mammillaria* include many popular houseplants. Instead of ridges, many mammillarias are covered in knobby, symmetrical bumps, known as tubercles, that hold the spine-bearing areoles at their tips. These cacti grow gradually into rounded clusters that may spread to 8 inches; most houseplant species rarely grow more than 6 inches tall.

Wonderfully woolly: The species known as old lady cactus (*Mammillaria hahniana*) and powder puff cactus

(*Mammillaria bocasana*) are among the mammillarias that cover themselves in silky bristles that give them the appearance of being covered in white hair. Don't be tempted to pet their pretty "fur"—there are also sturdy, hooked spines in those fuzzy tufts.

Rings of posies: Happy mammillarias that receive adequate bright light and cool winter rest will bloom when they reach maturity, around 4–5 years old for most species. Creamy yellow to white or red flowers form in a ring near the top of the plant in late spring.

RAT'S TAIL CACTUS (*APOROCACTUS FLAGELLIFORMIS*)

Much nicer than its name: The dangling stems of rat's tail cactus may reach 4–6 feet long as they trail prettily from a hanging basket. The ridged stems are covered in short, sharp spines that make it key to display this cactus where it won't be brushed by passersby.

Big bloomers: Hybrids of rat's tail cactus bear large, showy flowers in spring in shades of orange, purple, and pink.

More, please: Rat's tail cactus is easy to increase by taking cuttings from its trailing stems. Cut off a 6-inch tip or segment of stem and allow the cut edge(s) to dry for 2–3 days before sticking it into cactus potting soil. Make sure to "plant"

the cutting in the correct orientation, supporting it if needed to hold it upright while it roots.

SEA URCHIN CACTI (*ECHINOPSIS* HYBRIDS)

Barrels of fun: Echinopsis cacti grow clusters of classically barrel-shaped, ribbed globes that become columnar with age. Sea urchin cacti begin blooming when they are about 3 years old and are known for their large and fragrant flowers. Some echinopsis bloom only at night, but many hybrids have been developed to offer daylight flowers.

More, please: Echinopsis produce clusters of offsets that may be separated from the main plant in summer after flowering has stopped and planted in pots of their own.

Calatheas

(Calathea species and hybrids)

The beautiful foliage of the various houseplants in the genus *Calathea* have inspired a menagerie's worth of animal-themed identities: peacocks, rattlesnakes, and zebras among them. Calathea leaves may be elongated and lance-shaped or broadly oval, but typically are striped and spotted in shades of green, cream, and burgundy, with painterly markings that appear as brushstrokes of color. The undersides of the leaves may be pinkish to deep red or purple. Whether your own leafy lovely boasts a beastly identity or is content to go by the name "calathea," you're sure to appreciate it for its fancy foliage that remains attractive all year.

Date I brought you home: _____

What I loved about you from the start: _____

Milestones in your growth: _____

HELP ME GROW

▶ Place your calathea in a spot where it gets moderate to bright but always indirect or filtered light. Exposure to full sun risks scorching its pretty leaves.

▶ With origins in tropical rainforests, your calathea needs warmth and humidity. Give it a spot where temperatures range from 65–80°F and protect it from drafts and abrupt fluctuations.

▶ **WHEN THE HEAT IS ON:** Pay particular attention to maintaining moist air in the winter months when your home may be warm enough but far too dry for your calathea's comfort. Keep your calathea in a steamy bathroom or atop a pebble tray and mist regularly.

▶ A rich but well-drained potting mix of soil and peat will keep your calathea's roots comfy. Repot your plant in spring, moving it into a slightly larger container and refreshing its potting soil.

FEED ME

▶ Give frequent drinks during the active growth period from spring to early fall, watering with room-temperature filtered or distilled water or with rainwater to keep the potting soil evenly moist but not soggy. Water more moderately during the winter, allowing the top half inch of the soil to dry out between drinks.

▶ **WATCH WATER QUALITY:** Calatheas are sensitive about what's in their water. Giving them softened, fluoridated, or hard water can lead to leaf browning.

▶ Feed your calathea every 2–3 weeks from spring through summer with a fertilizer for foliage plants. Reduce feedings to once per month in the fall and winter.

LOVE ME

Summer outside: If your summers are warm and humid, your calathea may enjoy time outdoors, as long as temperatures don't fall below 60°F. Choose a shady location for your vacationing plant to avoid sunburn.

A meditative relation: Calatheas often are confused with the closely related prayer plant (*Maranta leuconeura*, page 171), a similarly colorful foliage plant that folds its pretty leaves at night. These plants enjoy similar conditions and easy communal care.

More, please: When your peacock plant turns into a flock that crowds the pot, you can divide it into smaller clumps. Take care to get some roots with every piece that you move into a new container and give extra TLC to the divided plants while they adjust to their new cribs. Mist foliage and put a plastic bag over each pot containing a new division, removing the cover after new roots have formed.

Cape primroses
(Streptocarpus hybrids)

A plant parent who is fond of flowers will appreciate the generous blooming behavior of Cape primroses, cousins of African violets with a similar inclination to produce flowers for several months if not all year round. The Cape primrose flower color palette includes pinks, purples, reds, blues, and white, as well as selections that are bicolored or with contrasting veins or spots. The pretty, velvety-looking flowers arise on stalks above an arching rosette of crinkly, elongated lance-shaped leaves that may be 10–12 inches long.

Date I brought you home: _____

What I loved about you from the start: _____

Milestones in your growth: _____

HELP ME GROW

▶ Bright to moderate, indirect or filtered light will satisfy your Cape primrose's needs. These beauties will bloom freely indoors and even in artificial light, as long as they get enough exposure to light each day.

AFRAID OF THE DARK: If your Cape primrose seems shy about flowering, it may be telling you that it's spending too much time in the dark. Cape primroses need at least 15 hours of light daily.

▶ Average to cool household temperatures (60–70°F) are comfortable for Cape primroses. More than a day or two below 55°F will induce a rest period of slower growth. At the warmer end of its preferred range, your Cape primrose will enjoy additional humidity from a pebble tray to keep it from developing crispy brown edges on its leaves.

▶ Well-drained, loose and airy potting mix in a pot that's slightly snug for your baby's size will keep its shallow roots happy. Repot in the spring, taking care to avoid planting too deeply.

FEED ME

▶ Water often enough to keep the soil evenly moist, allowing the top half inch of soil to dry out in between drinks. Setting the pot in tepid water and letting your baby take up water from the bottom helps avoid water puddling around the base of the leaves, which can cause rot. Limit bottom watering sessions to 30 minutes at a time and let excess water drain out of the pot afterward. If your Cape primrose goes into rest mode during cool, dim winter days, reduce watering accordingly, but never let its soil dry out to the point of wilting.

▶ It takes energy to provide a steady floral show. Feed your Cape primrose prodigy every 2–3 weeks with fertilizer designed for flowering houseplants.

LOVE ME

Read my leaves: Cape primrose's outer, lower leaves normally become brown and shriveled with age; clip them off to make way for fresh foliage. Spots on leaves may be caused by splashing water or liquid fertilizer or scorching from direct sun exposure in the summer. Pale foliage typically indicates too little light and/or a need for feeding. Snip off flowers as they begin to fade to urge baby to make more.

More, please: As with its African violet kin, you can increase your Cape primrose by rooting a cutting of a leaf and its short stem; remove about half of the leaf blade to avoid overburdening the cutting's developing roots.

Cast iron plant
(Aspidistra elatior)

In case the name "cast iron plant" doesn't alert you, the leafy green aspidistra is one tough houseplant. If your plant-parenting style is more Darwin than Dr. Spock, this is a great choice for you. This adaptable and durable plant will be okay if your travel schedule takes you away for a week or two at a time or if the brightest light in your apartment comes from opening the refrigerator. For first-time plant parents, cast iron plant can help you learn the basics of houseplant care and build your confidence for taking on more demanding adoptees.

Date I brought you home: _____

What I loved about you from the start: _____

Milestones in your growth: _____

HELP ME GROW

▶ Also called barroom plant because of its ability to survive in the low lighting of a tavern, aspidistra will grow in low to moderate light situations, including under artificial lights.

SAVE THE STRIPES AND SPOTS: Varieties of cast iron plant that have leaves marked with creamy to yellow stripes or spots need more light than their plain green kin. In dim lighting, the pretty markings of variegated forms tend to fade. Put your speckled or striped cast iron plant where it will receive indirect natural light.

▶ Cast iron plant can tolerate temperatures ranging from 45–85°F, so it's likely that your home environment will meet its needs. Like most houseplants, it will grow more slowly as the temperature drops and will need more attention to moisture when the temperature climbs. Its waxy leaves help it tolerate dry indoor air better than many houseplants do.

▶ Fill your cast iron plant's pot with a soil-based potting mix and forget about it. Your easy-care adoptee will appreciate being repotted in the spring after 3–4 years when you can treat it to fresh soil and a slightly larger pot.

FEED ME

▶ Water this self-sufficient plant lightly from spring into midsummer, allowing the potting soil to dry out two-thirds of the way down in between drinks. Cut back on the moisture even more heading into fall and winter.

DON'T DROWN ME: The one way a rookie plant parent may go astray with cast iron plant is by overwatering it. Make sure your plant's pot has good drainage and limit drinks to a minimum.

▶ Feed your cast iron plant sparingly, applying liquid houseplant fertilizer every 3–4 weeks in spring and summer and then every other month in fall and winter.

LOVE ME

Take a shine to me: Keep your cast iron plant looking its best by gently wiping its leathery leaves with a damp cloth to remove dust and give them a pleasing shine.

More, please: Cast iron plant grows from rhizomatous roots that you can divide. Separate a crowded clump in the spring, making sure that divisions have both roots and leafy shoots. Plant clumps in fresh potting soil in smallish pots. Avoid the temptation to spoil the divisions with fertilizer or overwatering.

Chinese evergreen
(Aglaonema commutatum)

Easygoing and willing to sparkle in spaces where the lighting is too low for many other houseplants, your Chinese evergreen will bask in modest care and modest light. With pretty color-brushed lance-shaped leaves that arch gracefully from low stems, this foliage plant will add an elegant accent to your home and earn a lasting place in your heart. Chinese evergreen's smooth, glossy leaves look as though they've been dabbed or speckled with colors, including silver, cream, yellow, and pink, over the top of their medium-green background.

Date I brought you home: _____

What I loved about you from the start: _____

Milestones in your growth: _____

HELP ME GROW

▶ Place your Chinese evergreen in a spot where it will receive low to moderate light, such as near a north-facing window.

NOT TOO BRIGHT: Direct sun is a no-no for Chinese evergreens. Strong light can scorch the foliage and spoil its good looks. Too much light overall may cause the foliage to grow pale.

▶ Your Chinese evergreen will be comfortable in average household temperatures and slightly above-average humidity. Set its pot on a pebble tray filled with water to boost humidity around the leaves, especially during the winter when the air in your home may be too dry for comfort.

▶ Soil-based potting mix in a pot that's slightly snug for your Chinese evergreen's size will hold its roots just right. Repot every couple of years as needed to reduce overcrowding in the container, but avoid moving into a pot that's too large.

FEED ME

▶ Water moderately while your lovely evergreen is actively growing, usually from spring through fall, letting the top inch of the potting soil dry out in between refreshing drinks. Keep things evenly and lightly moist in your plant's pot but avoid over- and underwatering, both of which can cause your plant to become sad and droopy.

▶ Feed every 4–6 weeks with house-plant fertilizer. Don't overserve your Chinese evergreen, lest it grow overly tall and gangly.

LOVE ME 🖤

Time to moisturize: Use a spray bottle to spritz the foliage every few days during the winter months when dry indoor air can stress your baby's leaves. Occasionally wipe the leaves gently with a damp cloth to keep them glossy and clean.

Share warmth: Don't let this darling take a chill from exposure to cold air. Chinese evergreens need reliable warmth and may develop unattractive yellow spotting in response to temperatures below 60°F.

Christmas cacti

(Schlumbergera hybrids)

Raising a Christmas cactus or one of its equally attractive holiday-affiliated kin is not the greatest challenge in plant parenthood, but it does require you to provide the specific conditions your lovely cactus needs to encourage it to bloom. Because it hails from the rainforest rather than the desert, your darling schlumbergera may not resemble your notions of what a cactus looks like, but it is a true cactus, with branching, flattened, segmented stems instead of leaves. In the fall, buds form at the end tips of the terminal segments, opening in winter into pendent pink blossoms.

Date I brought you home: _____

What I loved about you from the start: _____

Milestones in your growth: _____

HELP ME GROW

▶ Your baby enjoys basking in bright but indirect light from spring into fall. Direct summer sun can cause reddish discoloring of the stems; exposure to direct sunlight in winter is okay as long as air temperatures remain cool.

▶ Christmas cactus does well in average household temperatures (55–80°F) but benefits from seasonal adjustments.

SEASONAL SENSITIVITY: A shady spot outdoors where it can enjoy warmth and bright, filtered light is the perfect summer vacation for Christmas cactus. Let it stay outdoors until night temperatures hover around 50°F, then move your baby into a cool indoor room (55–65°F) to rest. After flowering, return it to a cool room for more rest until spring arrives.

▶ Potting soil amended with sand for drainage and enriched with leaf mold will satisfy your Christmas cactus. Its stems will dangle prettily over the sides of a hanging basket or a shallow container.

FEED ME

▶ Keep your Christmas cactus's soil lightly but evenly moist from spring through fall, serving it filtered or distilled water or rainwater. Let the top half inch of soil dry out between waterings, but watch for any signs of shriveling. Use a pebble tray to increase humidity. Reduce watering after flowering, but don't let the soil dry out entirely.

▶ Feed your Christmas cactus every 2–3 weeks with a fertilizer meant for flowering plants from spring into early fall. Reduce servings to once per month through the fall and winter.

LOVE ME

Rest to bloom: In the fall, place your cactus where it can rest in complete darkness. After buds have formed, move it to a place of honor. Avoid moving too much or re-orienting your Christmas cactus in relation to the light; any stress can cause it to drop its buds. After flowering, another rest is in order in cool, bright conditions with reduced watering until springtime.

Observing the holidays: Christmas cacti are winter bloomers that may or may not open their flowers promptly around yuletide. Thanksgiving cactus and Easter cactus (*Schlumbergera gaertneri*) have blooming habits corresponding roughly to those holidays.

More, please: Increase your cactus by taking cuttings of two to three stem segments in spring and summer. Let the cut edge dry for a few hours before sticking it into moistened potting soil just deep enough to support the cutting. Keep it out of bright light until new growth appears.

Citrus

(Citrus species and hybrids)

Your little orange may never produce enough fruits for a glass of fresh-squeezed, but these pretty bushes will deliver fragrant white flowers. In the right conditions, some citrus varieties can be productive, although indoor fruiting may prove more of a conversation piece than a significant harvest. The genus *Citrus* and its hybrids include lemons, limes, and oranges, as well as tangerines and grapefruits. All require similar care. Growing in a container will restrict many of them to indoor dimensions at least for a few years, and there are varieties that have been selected for small stature that makes them better suited to sharing your home.

Date I brought you home: _____

What I loved about you from the start: _____

Milestones in your growth: _____

You are a: _____

HELP ME GROW

▶ Bright sunlight for 4 or more hours a day will keep your citrus sweetie on track to be a productive as well as pretty family member. Turn the pot every few days.

SUMMER IN THE SUN: Spending the summer outdoors in a sunny situation will bring joy to any citrus. Make the move gradually from indoors to filtered light outdoors to full sun and back again in fall to avoid the shock of sudden changes.

▶ Average to warm (65–80°F) household temperatures will suit your citrus throughout the year. During the winter, its growth may slow in response to lower light levels and cooler temperatures down to 60°F will do it no harm. A pebble tray under the pot and occasional misting will help keep your plant comfy in dry indoor air.

▶ Plant your little citrus in a soil-based potting mixture, choosing a modest-sized container. Too much room in the pot increases the risk of overwatering and may discourage blooming. Graduate citrus into a larger pot size every year or two in spring until it maxes out on the size you are able to accommodate in your home.

BIG ENOUGH TO BLOSSOM: Some citrus will not bloom until they reach maturity and a 10-inch or larger container, while others, such as calamondin orange, may bloom and produce fruit while they are still quite small.

MIND THE THORNS: Citrus species are naturally thorny. Handle with care to avoid unpleasant encounters with prickly stems.

FEED ME

▶ Keep things lightly moist in your plant's pot from spring through summer. During fall and winter, cut back on drinks to allow the top half inch to inch of the potting soil to dry out in between waterings.

▶ Feed your citrus with a balanced plant food (or one labeled for tomatoes or cacti), serving it every 2–3 weeks during spring and summer. Reduce its meals to monthly in the fall and winter.

LOVE ME

CALAMONDIN ORANGE
(X CITROFORTUNELLA MITIS)

A *handsome hybrid:* Calamondin orange is a lovely and productive dwarf citrus tree, the product of a cross between kumquat and orange. In your home it will grow to 3–4 feet tall but will begin blooming and producing 1- to 2-inch-diameter orange fruits when it is just 2 years old. Watch small trees that begin blooming and bearing fruits, as you may need to thin the crop to prevent weighing down the branches.

Tart and tangy: The flavor of calamondin orange is tart like a lemon rather than sweet like the orange fruits it resembles. Use your harvest like lemons or in recipes that include added sweeteners.

Make like a bee: Help your calamondin orange in its journey from flowers to fruits by assisting the movement of pollen between flowers. Wriggle the tip of a small dry paintbrush in the middle of a flower, then move on to the next blossom until all have been dabbed with the brush.

KUMQUAT (*FORTUNELLA* SPECIES)

Similar to citrus: Close kin to citrus and partner in hybrids like calamondin orange, kumquats are small thorny trees that grow to about 4 feet tall in a container. Plants have leathery dark green foliage and greenish stems. Like citrus, they produce fragrant white flowers. The round to slightly oblong sweet-tart fruits ripen slowly to orange-yellow; they typically are eaten without removal of the peel.

MEYER LEMON (*CITRUS LIMON* 'MEYER', A.K.A. *CITRUS X MEYERI*)

A pretty little lemon: A hybrid citrus tree that stays small for indoor growing, Meyer lemon will give you a crop of pale, slightly sweet lemons for garnishing drinks and other citrusy applications. Even without its edible fruits, your Meyer lemon will enhance your home with fragrant flowers and attractive glossy foliage.

Humidity, please: If your little lemon starts losing flowers, it may be that the air in your home is too dry. Mist regularly while it's in bloom to increase the humidity, or give it a humidifier to make it comfortable while it blooms.

Wait for the ripe time: Citrus fruits do not ripen after they're harvested and indoor development progresses slowly. Be patient. Meyer lemons may take up to a year to fully ripen. Pick only when they are rich yellow and give slightly to the touch. Use shears to clip off ripe fruits and avoid breaking branches.

Croton

(Codiaeum variegatum var. pictum)

A colorful croton will bring a tropical note to your home with glossy, leathery leaves that may be spotted or streaked in reds, greens, and yellows, often with prominent contrasting veins. Beyond their bright and varying colors, croton leaves come in a wide array of shapes. Some selections bear smooth, broadly lance-shaped leaves, while others have foliage that is long and narrow, curled in fantastical corkscrews, twisted, crinkled, or irregularly lobed. Keep your croton happy with a bit of coddling and it will reward you by growing into a shrubby 2- to 3-foot-tall family member that looks handsome year-round.

Date I brought you home: _____

What I loved about you from the start: _____

Milestones in your growth: _____

HELP ME GROW

▶ Your croton needs abundant light to keep its leaf colors bright, but avoid placing it in direct sun.

JUST-RIGHT LIGHT: Finding a suitable location for your croton can be a bit tricky. With too little light, your croton may become pale and lose its lower leaves, while exposure to strong summer sun can scorch its foliage. Spending summer outdoors in a spot that gets filtered sunlight can be a color booster for a croton, but providing bright conditions for it indoors is important for its ongoing health and good looks.

▶ Consistency is key to being a good parent to a croton. Keep it comfortable with warm room temperatures that never drop below 60°F and a pebble tray to provide the humidity it loves. Drafts, dry indoor air, and abrupt temperature swings will make your croton sulky and prone to shedding its pretty leaves.

▶ Soil-based potting mix will keep your croton happy. Repot it in spring every year or two, but keep its container size slightly snug to prevent your tropical tot from outgrowing its space in your home.

FEED ME

▶ Water with tepid (never cold) water to maintain evenly moist (but not soggy) soil. In the winter, let the top half inch of the potting soil dry out between drinks.

▶ Nourish with a balanced fertilizer every 2–3 weeks from spring through summer. Reduce feedings to once a month in fall and winter.

LOVE ME

Look out for leaf loss: Nearly any adverse conditions—chilling, dry air, underwatering or overwatering—can cause your croton to drop some leaves. It will also naturally shed lower, older leaves. If leaf loss seems to affect more than the oldest leaves, check your care regimen and adjust accordingly.

Put a shine on me: Regularly wipe your croton's leaves with a damp cloth to keep them glossy and clean.

Handle with care: Crotons have milky sap that may cause skin irritation. Wear gloves when repotting or trimming to avoid unwanted contact with it.

Cryptanthus

(Cryptanthus bivittatus, Cryptanthus zonatus)

Flattened rosettes of colorfully striped or patterned, wavy foliage earn the various species of cryptanthus names such as earth star and zebra plant. Adopt one of these petite, low-growing bromeliads for its attractive leaves and you won't mind a bit that its botanical name, *Cryptanthus*, means "hidden flower." On the small side among bromeliads, cryptanthus are popular for growing in terrariums, where they enjoy the high humidity and their ribbonlike leaves contrast nicely with the fine-textured foliage of ferns.

Date I brought you home: _____

What I loved about you from the start: _____

Milestones in your growth: _____

HELP ME GROW

▶ Place your little earth star where it can shine. Bright light brings out the colors in cryptanthus foliage. Give it a spot near a sunny window, in a place where you can admire its starry display.

▶ Normal to warm household temperatures year-round will keep your cryptanthus cozy and comfortable. Provide extra humidity when home heating makes the air too dry for a bromeliad's comfort. Avoid drafts and chilly conditions below 55°F, which can damage its pretty leaves.

▶ Cryptanthus roots are small and wiry, meant for anchoring plants into rocky crevices or onto tree trunks and branches. Give your earth star a broad and shallow pot filled with a potting mix that combines peat moss or coir (coconut fiber) and leaf mold or potting soil in equal parts. You can also wrap its roots in sphagnum moss and mount it on a porous branch for display. Repot in fresh potting soil in spring every 3 years or as needed when offsets develop.

FEED ME

▶ Water with filtered or distilled water or with rainwater, enough to keep the potting soil lightly moist around the roots. Cut back on the drinks in the winter months but avoid letting the roots dry out completely.

▶ In spring and summer, nourish your cryptanthus by "foliar feeding" once a month, sprinkling the leaves with a dilute liquid fertilizer.

LOVE ME

Colors of cryptanthus: While its flowers may be "meh" shades of greenish white, your cryptanthus can truly stand out for spectacular foliar colors. Earth star (*Cryptanthus bivittatus*) foliage has toothed edges and colorful stripes that run the length of each wavy leaf in shades of pink, red, purple, orange, or cream. The horizontal stripes of zebra plant (*Cryptanthus zonatus*) alternate from deep green to burgundy and cream, adorning wavy, spidery leaves that reach 6–8 inches long. Bright light is the key to colorful cryptanthus; colors and striping may fade to green if light levels are too low.

More, please: Like most bromeliads, after it blooms, your cryptanthus will gradually die back. Continue to care for it and watch for "pups"—offsets forming around the base of the original. These may be gently separated from their parent and given pots of their own when they grow to be about half the size of the parent plant. Cover the containers of newly planted pups with a plastic bag to provide humid conditions while they settle into their new homes.

Date palms

(Phoenix roebelenii, Phoenix canariensis)

If you have room in your home and in your heart for a showy 6-footer that may spread its fronds out to 5 feet wide, a date palm may be just what you need. Two species, Canary Island date palm and dwarf or miniature date palm, are widely grown as houseplants. These smaller relatives of the palms that produce edible dates will not yield fruits when grown indoors, but their arching stems of long, narrow pinnae (leaflets) and bumpy stems will create the effect of a tropical oasis.

Date I brought you home: _____

What I loved about you from the start: _____

Milestones in your growth: _____

HELP ME GROW

▶ Your date palm will bask in bright, indirect or filtered light.

GO MOBILE: Date palms grow outdoors where winters are mild and frost-free. Yours will enjoy spending summer in a sunny spot on your balcony or patio, if you are able to move it. Placing its pot on castors can help keep your date palm mobile even when it grows large, and allows you to turn it occasionally for even light exposure on all sides of the plant.

▶ Average household temperatures (65–75°F) will meet your date palm's needs. If possible, a winter rest in cool conditions (50–55°F) is beneficial, but avoid exposure to temperatures below 50°F.

NO DRAFTS OR DRY AIR: Brown leaf tips may indicate that your date palm is chilled or dry from indoor heating. Make sure it's out of the range of heat vents and provide a pebble tray and/or occasional misting to boost the humidity in its space. Use scissors to trim off brown tips.

▶ Mix a soil-based potting mix with sand for your date palm's comfort and support. Repot in spring every 2–3 years, increasing the size of the pot by an inch or two until you reach 10–12 inches for a date palm that's no more than 4 feet tall. Larger date palms may be too heavy and fragile to repot easily; apply fresh potting mix to the top of their containers in the spring.

FEED ME

▶ Water regularly in the spring and summer to maintain even moisture. Let the top inch of the potting mix dry out between waterings. Reduce watering in cooler conditions when your date palm is not actively growing, but don't let it dry out completely.

▶ Feed your pretty date palm with a balanced houseplant fertilizer every 3–4 weeks from spring through late summer. Pause feedings during fall and winter.

LOVE ME

How mini? Miniature or pygmy date palm (*Phoenix roebelenii*, also called robellini) is small compared to other date palms but on the large side by most houseplant standards. Indoors in a container it will grow slowly and may remain under 3 feet tall, but it has the potential to grow to 6 feet or more. Canary Island date palm (*Phoenix canariensis*) will reach 6 feet tall when grown in a container.

Handle with care: Don't be fooled by the delicate appearance of your miniature date palm's fine-textured fronds. The base of each leaflet bears spines that pose a hazard to unprotected handlers. As your date palm's lower fronds naturally fade with age, snip them off at the base as they turn brown and begin to droop, wearing gloves to protect your hands while you work.

Dieffenbachias, dumb cane
(Dieffenbachia species and hybrids)

Handsomely patterned and color-splotched foliage borne on upright, cane-like stems creates lush, tropical-looking plants that may grow 2–3 feet tall and wide, depending on variety. Over a base color of green, dieffenbachia's broadly oval leaves may be marked with white, cream, or yellow, and markings may include irregular spots, contrasting-colored veins, or tidy stripes of color. In a bright room, a happy dieffenbachia's bold leaves will provide an attractive contrast to the fine textures of palms or ferns.

Date I brought you home: _____

What I loved about you from the start: _____

Milestones in your growth: _____

HELP ME GROW

▶ Bright but filtered or indirect light is best for your dear dumb cane from spring through fall. In the winter, it will enjoy as much light as you can provide, including direct sun exposure.

▶ Dieffenbachias need warmth and humidity to keep them cozy and will become sulky and inclined to shed leaves if exposed to temperatures below 60°F or even the occasional chilly draft. Mist your plant's pretty leaves and place its pot on a tray of wet pebbles to provide the humid air it craves.

▶ Soil-based potting mix will keep your dieffenbachia happy. Repot every year or two in spring while it is small and still growing, increasing the size of its pot until it reaches an 8- to 10-inch container.

FEED ME

▶ Water to maintain evenly moist (but not soggy) soil. In the winter, let the top half inch of the potting soil dry out between drinks.

▶ Nourish with a balanced fertilizer every 2–3 weeks from spring through summer. Reduce feedings to once a month in fall and winter.

LOVE ME

Don't be dumb: Wonder why your pretty plant is known as dumb cane? Dieffenbachias have calcium oxalate crystals in their sap that can cause irritation and swelling in the mouth and throat of anyone foolish enough to take a bite. The resulting adverse effect makes it tough to talk—and possibly to breathe—hence dumb cane. Keep this cautionary tale in mind when choosing a spot for your own darling dumb cane and position it out of the reach of curious kids and pets.

Tidy up: Regularly wipe your dieffenbachia's leaves with a damp cloth to keep them glossy and clean. Lower leaves naturally fade and fall off as your plant grows; snip them off when they begin to turn yellow.

Special care: Wear gloves and/or take care to wash your hands after handling your dieffenbachia to avoid unpleasant encounters with its toxic sap.

Dracaenas

(Dracaena species and hybrids)

Diverse dracaenas produce effects ranging from fanciful to formal with their colorfully stripy ribbonlike leaves arching from stems. This group of foliage plants includes forms to fit almost any décor and care requirements even novice plant parents can handle. Most dracaenas produce their pointed leaves in a spiral pattern around a woody stem that culminates in a rosette of foliage. As plants age, they tend to lose their lower leaves, exposing a stem decorated by triangular leaf scars; the resulting effect is palmlike, but easier to care for.

Date I brought you home: _____

What I loved about you from the start: _____

Milestones in your growth: _____

HELP ME GROW

▶ Indirect bright to moderate lighting will help your dracaena maintain its pretty colors, and it will be happiest if it receives a couple hours of filtered sunlight daily.

DON'T KEEP ME IN THE DARK: While your dracaena can survive in low light, it won't grow up to make you proud without adequate lighting. Pale leaves and fading stripes are signs that conditions are too dim.

▶ Dracaenas need normal household temperatures (65–75°F) and moderate humidity. Give yours a moist pebble tray and occasional spritzes with a mister to keep it happy. Avoid temperatures of 60°F and lower, which can give your dracaena a chill and cause it to lose its leaves.

▶ Nestle your dracaena's roots in a soil-based potting mix in a modest-sized pot. Narrow-leaved, smaller species will be happy in fairly snug containers, while broad-leaved dracaenas appreciate a bigger pot that can better support their size. Repot in spring every year or two, increasing container size until your dracaena reaches a satisfying size.

FEED ME

▶ Water regularly to keep the soil evenly moist, but steer clear of overwatering and soggy conditions.

▶ Nourish with a balanced fertilizer every 2–3 weeks from spring through summer. Reduce feedings to once a month in fall and winter.

LOVE ME

Celebrate rural roots: The handsome corn plant (*Dracaena fragrans* 'Massangeana') has arching, broad, pointed leaves with lengthwise yellow stripes that bear a resemblance to the leaves of corn in the field. This effect is heightened by the dracaena's sturdy, upright habit; mature plants may reach 6 feet tall.

Raise a dragon: The narrow leaves of Madagascar dragon tree (*Dracaena marginata*) are dark green with thin red-purple edges; the variety 'Tricolor' has narrow stripes of pink and cream running the length of its leaves. A slender, easygoing dracaena, your little dragon tree can grow up to 5 feet tall to deliver an attractive vertical accent in your home with woody stems topped by a pleasingly quirky mop of spiky colorful leaves.

Not for pets: Although their grassy foliage may attract nibbles from your fur-family members, dracaenas contain substances that are toxic to dogs and cats and should be placed out of pets' reach.

Echeverias

(Echeveria species and hybrids)

As a group, echeverias are petite, rosette-forming succulents with charming personalities and easy-growing habits. Their thick leaves may be rounded, blunt-tipped, or acutely pointed, and in shades of blue-green, red, pink, or purple, sometimes with contrasting colors at the tips or leaf edges, and their smooth leaf surfaces typically are covered with a waxy, whitish "bloom." If you have limited space with a sunny exposure, perch a pot (or two or more) topped with an adorable echeveria where you can admire the intricately arranged symmetry of its fleshy foliage. While a mature echeveria will bloom if its light and care needs are fulfilled, the floral display of these plants is considered secondary to the reliable good looks of the leaves.

Date I brought you home: _____

What I loved about you from the start: _____

Milestones in your growth: _____

HELP ME GROW

▶ Abundant bright light, including some direct sun, keeps an echeveria's rosette of fleshy leaves looking its finest.

LET THE SUN SHINE: Summer in a sunny spot outdoors may cause your baby to blush with delight. Many varieties develop rosy hints on their leaves when exposed to strong light. Make moves from indoors to full sun gradually.

▶ Normal to warm room temperatures (65–85°F) while it is actively growing will satisfy your echeveria. In fall and winter, introduce a period of rest in bright light and cooler temperatures (55–70°F).

▶ Potting mix that is about one-quarter coarse sand provides good drainage. These low-growing plants look attractive in broad, shallow containers. Repot every 2 years in the spring. Top the potting soil with a layer of fine gravel or coarse sand to keep moisture away from the base.

FEED ME

▶ Water lightly, allowing the top inch of the potting soil to dry out in between drinks during the spring and summer. If your echeveria covers the entire surface, water by setting the pot in a shallow saucer of water and letting it take up water from the bottom until the mix in the pot is evenly moistened. Don't leave your baby to drink for more than a couple hours and make sure to let excess water drain. If your echeveria is resting in cool conditions in fall and winter, water it just enough to keep the soil from drying out.

NO SPOTS AND ROT: Avoid sprinkling the leaves or pouring water into the rosette, where it can cause rotting at the crown of your echeveria.

▶ Feed your succulent with a fertilizer meant for cacti, diluting it to half strength and serving every 2–3 weeks during spring and summer. Reduce feedings to once a month in fall and winter.

LOVE ME

Be gentle: Plump succulent foliage is tender and prone to breaking if it gets bumped. The waxy bloom on your echeveria's leaves can rub off when plants are handled, leaving spots that are at risk of sunburn or moisture loss. Handle gently when repotting, and avoid placing in a spot where bumps are likely to occur.

More, please: Echeveria are sometimes called hens and chicks, a common name also given to the more cold-hardy sempervivums. This name refers to their habit of producing small offsets, "chicks," around the base of the parent plant, the "hen." These may be gently separated and given pots of their own—easiest while the chicks are still small.

English ivy

(Hedera helix)

Trailing stems of English ivy produce a cascade of starry leaves that will drape attractively from a hanging basket or nestle at the base of a compatible upright container plant. Pretty, vigorous, and pliant, your ivy may also be guided to grow over a trellis or topiary form to take on almost any shape you wish. The broad array of English ivy varieties includes those with colorful leaf markings in silvery white or golden yellow, types with petite, sharply lobed leaves, and others with broader, more rounded foliage. English ivy tolerates cooler conditions than many houseplants, making it a good candidate for dressing up a drafty spot near an entrance or an unheated enclosed porch or sunroom.

Date I brought you home: _____

What I loved about you from the start: _____

Milestones in your growth: _____

HELP ME GROW

▶ Bright, indirect lighting is best for your ivy, particularly if it has variegated leaves.

FADE TO GREEN: In less than bright light conditions, the pretty spots and splashes of color on variegated English ivy may fade to plain green and vines may become stretched and less leafy. While varieties with unmarked foliage can grow in moderate lighting, all varieties are better in a bright location and variegated ivies will even enjoy a few hours of direct sun daily.

▶ Your English ivy will grow happily on the cool side of normal household temperatures. These sturdy plants can tolerate temperatures as low as 35°F but will be quite satisfied with ranges from 50–65°F. In winter, a cool rest period in a bright but rather chilly location will do your ivy good.

BE CONSISTENT: Wide temperature fluctuations can be upsetting to your ivy, as can overly warm conditions. Increase humidity by misting the leafy vines when the temperature exceeds 70°F. Ivies that are overheated may grow spindly; dry air can cause edges to brown.

▶ Plant your ivy in a soil-based potting mixture amended with perlite for good drainage. Increase the pot size of young plants whenever their roots begin to crowd their container. A 10-inch hanging basket may hold four to six small plants.

FEED ME

▶ Water English ivy moderately to maintain even soil moisture. Allow the top inch of potting soil to dry out between drinks. Water less frequently in winter without letting the soil dry out completely.

▶ Serve your ivy monthly with a fertilizer for foliage plants—meals that have more nitrogen than other ingredients.

LOVE ME

Provide parental guidance: English ivy may produce small aerial rootlets along its stems that allow it to root when it encounters a likely spot, but you should direct its growth if you want it to cover a topiary form or clamber up a trellis. Use twist ties or clips to fasten its vines where you want them to grow.

Sharing means caring: If your ivy shares quarters in a container with another houseplant, such as at the base of a treelike plant sibling, make sure you're providing for both plants' water and fertilizer needs, lest your pretty combo turn into a battle for resources that leaves both looking haggard.

More, please: You can expand your ivy family members quite easily by taking 3- to 4-inch cuttings from the tips of vines and rooting them in water or moist seed-starting mix.

False aralia

(Plerandra elegantissima, a.k.a. Dizygotheca elegantissima)

The toothed leaflets of false aralia fan out attractively from a central leaf stalk. Each 3- to 4-inch-long leaflet starts out a coppery reddish color but changes to dark green in the light. The leaf stalks and central stem are slender and greenish, mottled with white, and the overall effect is feathery and lacy. You—or guests in your home—may also note the leaves' resemblance to those of cannabis, but there is no relationship between your false aralia and marijuana. False aralia grows slowly to reach 5–6 feet tall.

Date I brought you home: _____

What I loved about you from the start: _____

Milestones in your growth: _____

HELP ME GROW

▶ Provide your false aralia a spot in bright but filtered or indirect sunlight to help it grow satisfyingly bushy. Direct sun may make leaf edges turn brown.

▶ Keep things cozy (65–85°F) for this lacy darling that appreciates warm temperatures year-round and will sulk if temps drop below 60°F. Give false aralia a moist pebble tray and mist frequently to satisfy its hankering for humid air.

▶ Use a soil-based potting mix in a modest-sized pot relative to your false aralia's size. Repot in spring every year or two, keeping the roots slightly snug in the container until you have moved baby into an 8- to 10-inch pot. Refresh the potting soil on the surface in spring once maximum container size is reached.

FEED ME

▶ Water thoroughly when you give your false aralia a drink, then let the top inch of its soil dry out before the next refreshment. Soggy soil is not desirable, but never let things get completely dried out in the pot.

▶ In spring and summer, nourish your aralia with a balanced fertilizer applied every 2–3 weeks. Feed monthly during fall and winter.

LOVE ME ♥

Provide calm: A change in location or exposure to chilly temperatures can cause your false aralia to shed its pretty leaves. Make moves in spring and summer when your little one is actively growing and better able to recover. Protect it from chills and keep a close eye on humidity during the winter when dry indoor air can cause leaves to become dry and fall off.

Group dynamics: False aralias typically grow upright with a single stem and can seem rather spindly as a result. Putting a few plants in a single pot helps create a bushier effect than a single false aralia on its own. Match your false aralia's feathery foliage and upright attitude with the more substantial presence of plants such as Chinese evergreen, dieffenbachia, or fiddle-leaf fig.

Ferns

If you're fond of *Jurassic Park* and *The Land Before Time*, you may relish the idea of a fern as a plant companion. The bushy fronds can create a cozy yet exotic junglelike atmosphere in your home. Ferns grow in the wild around the globe and are accordingly diverse. Those that grow naturally in temperate climates do not adapt well to indoor living, but many of the tropical species can be brought into your home and your heart. Your frond child will not bring you flowers but a fern's beautiful foliage can more than make up for the absence of blossoms.

Date I brought you home: _____

What I loved about you from the start: _____

Milestones in your growth: _____

You are a: _____

HELP ME GROW

▶ Medium to bright, filtered or indirect light satisfies most ferns' lighting needs. Ferns are adapted to life in shady conditions under leafy canopies and may suffer scorched foliage in direct sun. The exception is during the winter months when a few hours of exposure to weak morning sun can be beneficial.

DO THE TWIST: Uneven development can occur if your fern always faces the same direction. To encourage well-rounded growth, turn your fern's pot about a quarter turn twice a week.

▶ Average to cool (60–75°F) household temperatures will keep most ferns comfortable. The ferns that do best in a household environment are ones that come from warm climates. More important than warmth is humidity; ferns lose moisture through their leafy fronds and suffer when indoor heating makes the air around them dry and warm. Pebble trays and regular misting both are recommended for happy, healthy ferns.

▶ Forest floor–dwelling ferns like to sink their rather shallow roots into a growing medium that is rich in organic matter and well drained. For epiphytes, amend potting mix with an equal amount of peat moss, leaf mold, coarse sand, or perlite; for terrestrial ferns, use a soil-based mix amended with leaf mold.

Most ferns are shallow-rooted and need a shallow pan or half-deep pot. Repot ferns in the spring, checking for healthy, often light-colored, roots and pruning out any dead, blackened roots.

FEED ME

▶ Ferns can be thirsty children, but many dislike having soggy soil around their roots. Water often to maintain evenly moist conditions.

DON'T BE FOOLED: Peat-based potting mixes that dry out completely can be difficult to remoisten and may deceive you by feeling damp on the surface while roots dry out deeper in the pot. If your fern has dried out and water seems to run right through its container, submerge the pot to its rim in tepid water for just a couple of minutes, then lift it out and let the excess drain away.

NO COLD SHOWERS: For misting and watering, your fern will appreciate its moisture at room temperature.

▶ Your fern's nutritional needs will depend upon its type and the time of year. In general, ferns need modest feeding in spring and summer when they are actively growing and somewhat less when growth slows in fall and winter. Unless you're serving a fern-specific fertilizer blend, dilute feedings to half the dose recommended on the label.

LOVE ME 💜

BIRD'S NEST FERN
(*ASPLENIUM NIDUS*)

Large-leaved and lovely: The broad, bright green fronds of bird's nest fern may run counter to your idea of what a fern looks like, but this pretty epiphyte tolerates household conditions well and can be a long-lasting companion in your home or office.

Out of the nest: Bird's nest fern gets its name from the fibrous brown crown at the center of its rosette of wavy, ribbonlike leaves. New fronds curl up from this central nest and a healthy plant may grow to 18 inches tall and wide. Your bird's nest fern will do fine with moderate lighting and can survive with less humidity than many ferns but will appreciate a moist pebble tray to keep it from getting too dry. When watering, avoid pouring water into your fern's rosette.

Freshen my fronds: New foliage is delicate when it first unfurls from the central "nest" but the older fronds benefit from occasional cleaning. Spritz them with tepid water and then wipe gently with a damp cloth. Outer fronds naturally turn brown with age and may be trimmed off with scissors.

BRAKE FERN, RIBBON FERN, TABLE FERN (*PTERIS* SPECIES)

Pumped for brakes: A pretty brake fern will wave its fingerlike pinnae in open-palmed clusters atop slender stems. The various species differ in the size and color of these sometimes wavy or ruffled leaflets but most grow to 6–12 inches tall with a similar spread.

Delicate but durable: Your brake fern may look dainty but will get along well with modest care. Keep it in bright but indirect light and coolish (60–70°F) conditions for maximum happiness; boost the humidity when the temperature rises or when winter heating makes things dry.

More, please: Brake ferns grow slowly and may be repotted every couple of years or as needed. If you want more of your own pretty brake fern, divide it in spring. Cut its shallow rhizome into sections bearing fronds and roots and pot them up in a fresh, moist mix of peat and potting soil.

BUTTON FERN
(*PELLAEA ROTUNDIFOLIA*)

A pretty, cool customer: Arching 12-inch stems clad in pairs of small dark green rounded pinnae give button fern an airy but orderly feel. This easy-care fern puts up with cooler conditions (as low as 50°F) than some and won't shiver if it encounters an occasional draft. Extended time below 55°F may slow your button fern's growth; water sparingly during such a rest period. If things are warmer (70°F and above) where your button fern grows, pay close attention to supplying humidity with daily misting.

Button up or down: Your button fern will look pretty with its elegant fronds extended from a hanging basket or in a low pot at the base of a larger, bolder-textured plant. Repotting is needed only occasionally when its roots become crowded; you can divide the rhizomes in spring to increase your button collection, replanting the sections horizontally just below the surface of fresh potting mix.

HOLLY FERN (*CYRTOMIUM FALCATUM*)

No berries, though: The glossy pointed pinnae of a holly fern make its fronds look much more like sprigs of festive greenery than the usual ferny foliage. A handsome holly fern will be happy in a spot near a bright window but will make do in moderate lighting. You can keep this fern where temperatures are on the chilly side, and it is better than most ferns at tolerating low humidity. Even so, if it lives in a warm spot in your home, it will appreciate accommodations for moistening the air around it, especially during the winter heating season.

Tough enough: In mild climates, holly fern grows outdoors and is used as a shady groundcover. Plants may grow to 24 inches tall and spread gradually by shallow rhizomes. Your holly fern will enjoy spending summer outdoors in a shaded location. An occasional shower will help freshen up its shiny fronds.

More, please: Holly fern grows at a moderate pace and may be repotted and divided in spring when its roots become crowded in their container. Create more plants by separating sections of rhizome with three to four fronds attached and planting them just below the surface of moistened potting mixture.

MAIDENHAIR FERN (*ADIANTUM RADDIANUM*)

Fancy but finicky: Fine-textured with fronds bearing delicate triangular pinnae, maidenhair fern is among the most popular and common ferns sold as houseplants but not one of the easiest to please. Your pretty maidenhair might well be called Goldilocks for its need to have conditions "just right." This fern needs bright light but never direct sun, evenly lightly moist soil but never soggy or very dry, and abundant humidity. It will tolerate temperatures as low as 50°F but dislikes drafts and temperature fluctuations; its humidity needs increase at temperatures above 75°F.

Fronds in need: If your maidenhair fern is unhappy, it will show in those pretty fronds. Yellowing foliage may indicate overwatering or exposure to abrupt changes in temperature. Pale fronds can result from too much light— and may also display scorching—or too little light or may mean that your fern needs feeding. Brown, dry leaves are signs of low humidity, drafts, too much sun, or dry potting soil. Adjust your care regimen to correct these problems, and use scissors to snip off afflicted fronds to make way for new growth.

Happy when humid: Because humidity is important to your maidenhair fern's happiness, consider making it a resident of a steamy bathroom or growing it in a terrarium. If you find a spot where your maidenhair fern thrives, keep it there—changing locations may also disrupt a fern's demeanor.

POLYPODY FERN, HARE'S FOOT FERN (*PHLEBODIUM AUREUM*, A.K.A. *POLYPODIUM AUREUM*)

Ruffled flat fronds: Another fern with fuzzy "feet" creeping across the surface of its pot, a polypody fern bears leafy pinnae that are flattened with wavy edges. Its furry rhizomes are orange-brown or white and tend to grow around the inner edge of its pot.

Easy-growing and tidy: Your polypody fern likes bright lighting (no full sun) and daily misting to provide humid conditions. A weekly application of a dilute liquid fertilizer will help keep its rather abundant foliage looking good. While it boasts a colorful furry rhizome like the davallia ferns, a polypody fern may hide its hare's foot from view with lots of leaves. Polypody foliage tends to shed less than more fine-textured ferns.

More, please: You can make more polypody ferns by taking cuttings of the rhizomes as described for rabbit's foot fern (page 119). Repot your polypody in spring when the rhizomes have grown to cover the surface of the container. Choose a broad pot that gives this fern room to stretch its "feet" and plant in a mixture of potting soil and leaf mold.

RABBIT'S FOOT FERN, DEER'S FOOT FERN, SQUIRREL'S FOOT FERN (*DAVALLIA* SPECIES)

Animal or vegetable? When you really want a pet but need to settle for a plant, one of the animal-themed davallia ferns may be the perfect compromise. These ferns produce lacy triangles of finely divided pinnae from creeping rhizomes that are covered by hairlike rusty brown to silvery gray scales. The look of these fuzzy structures, which grow atop the soil and over the edge of a davallia fern's container, is similar to the furry feet of various animals.

Arachnophobes beware: another common name for rabbit's foot fern (*Davallia fejeensis*) is spider fern.

Put my feet up: A hanging basket or a broad shallow pot lets your ferny friend show off its fuzzy rhizomes. Rabbit's foot fern and its kin enjoy conditions similar to those preferred by maidenhair ferns but are a little more relaxed about soil moisture and humidity.

More, please: Repot every 2–3 years in spring, using a mixture of potting soil and peat moss. You can increase your furry-footed fern by taking a 2- to 3-inch cutting from the tip of a fuzzy rhizome and pinning it to the surface of a pot of moistened peat moss and perlite mix. Cover the container with a plastic bag to conserve moisture and place it in bright, indirect light and cool conditions. Do not cover the rhizomes with potting soil—they will rot.

Rabbit's foot fern

Ficus, fig
(Ficus species)

Several popular houseplants belong to the fig genus and are noteworthy for the widely differing characteristics of these closely related plants. Three of the ficus described here—weeping fig, fiddle-leaf fig, and rubber plant—are treelike, with effects ranging from graceful to bold. The fourth ficus, creeping fig, is a fine-textured climbing vine that may trail from a basket or climb up a trellis. Nurturing a ficus requires specific care, but when you find the one that's right for you, you'll discover that your own little fig is so easy to love.

Date I brought you home: _____

What I loved about you from the start: _____

Milestones in your growth: _____

You are a: _____

HELP ME GROW

▶ Moderate to bright, indirect light satisfies most ficus's needs. Turn your treelike ficus every few days in relation to its main light source to prevent lopsided development.

HELP COLORS SHINE: If your ficus has variegated foliage, place it where it will get bright light and maybe even an hour or two of morning sun. Without enough light, those pretty white- or color-splashed leaves may fade to plain green. If you lack a sufficiently bright window location, consider supplementing with artificial light.

▶ Your ficus will be comfortable in normal to warm household conditions and can adapt *gradually* to temperatures ranging from 60–85°F. Abrupt changes in temperature can cause distress, which typically means leaf loss. In very warm conditions, provide additional humidity, especially for weeping fig.

▶ Choose a soil-based potting mix that offers good drainage for your ficus and give it a pot that is slightly snug. Keep balance in mind when selecting a container for a rubber plant or fiddle-leaf fig to ensure its substantial top growth doesn't outweigh the base and make it prone to tipping.

FEED ME

▶ Tepid, unsoftened water is a good choice for moistening the soil and misting the foliage of any ficus. Watering needs vary by species, with fiddle-leaf and creeping figs being thirstier and weeping fig and rubber plant in need of drier conditions.

▶ Feed rubber plant and weeping and creeping figs monthly with balanced houseplant fertilizer from spring through fall; do not fertilize in winter. Fiddle-leaf fig appreciates more nitrogen to support its large leaves and will benefit from a plant food for foliage plants, diluted to half strength and served monthly from spring through late summer.

LOVE ME

CREEPING FIG (*FICUS PUMILA*)

A *delicate climber:* The tidy heart-shaped leaves of creeping fig are thin compared to those of its ficus cousins and this fig has a greater need for watering and humidity than others of its genus. Water regularly in spring and summer to keep its soil lightly moist; let the surface dry out between drinks in the winter. Creeping fig can tolerate relatively low light and cooler than normal tempera-tures but needs bright, indirect light and average warmth to put on new growth.

Mist the foliage to keep it comfortably humid. Creeping figs with white-marked leaves make attractive topiaries.

Help me take shape: Give your creeping fig a topiary shape filled with moss and guide its creeping tendrils where you want them to grow. Aerial rootlets form along its trailing stems, allowing it to climb over a small trellis or any other shape you provide. Use scissors to snip off stems that grow out of bounds.

More, please: You can take cuttings in the spring from the tips of creeping fig's stems and stick them in moist potting soil to root.

FIDDLE-LEAF FIG (*FICUS LYRATA*)

Fiddle-dee-dee: The broad, paddle-shaped, dark green leaves of fiddle-leaf fig may be more than a foot long and over 8 inches wide and are produced from an upright, woody trunk. With time, your fiddle-leaf may grow to 6 feet tall. Its needs are similar to those of weeping fig, but it likes lightly moist soil throughout the growing season and benefits from a fertilizer that contains micronutrients.

Keeping clean: Fiddle-leaf fig's big leaves have lots of surface area for trapping dust. Spritz them with your mister and wipe gently clean with a damp cloth to keep them looking their best.

Handle with care: Fiddle-leaf figs have milky sap that may cause skin irritation.

RUBBER PLANT (*FICUS ELASTICA*)

Light, bright: Your pretty rubber plant will get along in moderate lighting but it needs bright lighting to make new growth and maintain its treelike form. To encourage upward progress, give it a boost with a lamp if you don't have the necessary bright window for it. Rubber plant grows slowly indoors to a height of 6 feet or more. To promote branching, clip off the growing point in spring. Rubber plants with variegated leaves marked with pink, burgundy, or yellow require more light than the green-leaved species to maintain their colorful foliage.

Let me shine: Keep your rubber plant's leaves looking fine with regular wipe-downs with a damp cloth to remove dust and add a glossy shine. Support each broad, oval leaf with one hand underneath while wiping the top surface to prevent breakage.

Handle with care: The name "rubber plant" is not a joke. This ficus (all ficus, actually) has milky latex flowing in its veins. Snap off a glossy leaf or snip the main stem and a flow of sap will follow. Avoid getting it on your skin as it can cause irritation.

WEEPING FIG (*FICUS BENJAMINA*)

Give me time: It's easy to fall in love with this small tree's graceful weeping branches clad in slender, oval, dark green leaves. And it's all too easy to cause those pretty leaves to fall, as leaf loss is weeping fig's go-to response to almost any environmental stress. As the adult in the room, it's up to you to make sure your weeping fig's needs are satisfied and to respond calmly and patiently when leaf shedding occurs. Don't rush to make changes if leaves drop in the wake of repotting or a move to a new location; if all other needs are being met, continue to provide appropriate care and give your ficus time to adjust.

Why I weep: Some leaf loss is normal in the fall when weeping fig may shed up to one-fifth of its foliage as growth slows. At other times, falling leaves may result from over- or underwatering, dry air, cold drafts, repotting, or a change of location.

Place your weeping fig where it gets bright, indirect light and perhaps a bit of direct sun if it has variegated leaves. Keep it out of cold drafts and away from the warm air of heat vents. Let the upper 1–2 inches of its potting soil dry out between drinks when your ficus is actively growing. Water even more sparingly in winter but mist the foliage regularly and use a moist pebble tray to provide humidity.

Repot or not: Move your weeping fig into a bigger container only when roots appear at drainage holes or on the soil surface. Repot in spring before new growth begins. Resist the temptation to overwater or feed your ficus after repotting. Give it time to settle its roots—and perhaps shed a leaf or two—before fertilizing.

Weeping fig

Grape ivy
(Cissus rhombifolia)

Give it a spot in your home and grape ivy will quickly wrap its tendrils around your heart with its easy-growing nature. Its glossy evergreen leaves are made up of three leaflets with toothed edges. Viewed collectively, they resemble the broader rhomboid foliage of true grapes. Young leaves open with a silvery, fuzzy coating and mature to shiny dark green; the leaves are carried on short stalks that arise from jointed brown vines. Grape ivy will grow vigorously in good conditions and may stretch its vines 2 feet or more in a year's time.

Date I brought you home: _____

What I loved about you from the start: _____

Milestones in your growth: _____

HELP ME GROW

▶ Medium to bright, indirect lighting will suit your grape ivy. Growth will be best in bright conditions, but grape ivy can adapt to life under modest and artificial light. Avoid direct sun, which can injure the foliage.

▶ Normal warm room temperatures (65–80°F) during spring and summer let grape ivy put on good growth. A winter rest in cooler conditions (55–65°F) will do it good.

▶ Well-drained potting soil mixed with peat moss is a cozy choice for keeping your grape ivy comfy. Repot in spring, moving up a pot size until it reaches an 8- to 10-inch container, then refresh the surface of the potting soil in subsequent years.

FEED ME

▶ Keep your grape ivy's potting mix lightly and evenly moist from spring into early fall. Reduce watering in winter to let the top inch of soil dry out before delivering the next drink.

▶ Nourish with a balanced fertilizer every 3–4 weeks from spring through fall. Pause feedings during the winter while your grape ivy is resting.

LOVE ME

Happy to hang: Grape ivy looks handsome in a hanging basket and will dangle prettily in a wide range of conditions. If its vines get too unruly, give them a trim with scissors to promote more branching, bushy growth.

A clever climber: Tendrils help grape ivy climb and its vines may be trained up a trellis or bark post to create a vertical effect. Grape ivy vines may grow to 6 feet long.

Haworthia, zebra plant

(Haworthia fasciata)

A petite, stripy succulent with pointy-tipped fleshy leaves that grow in a tidy rosette, haworthia is one of seemingly countless houseplants that also go by the name "zebra plant." Whatever you call this adaptable sprout, you'll find it makes an easy-care companion that will perch prettily on your windowsill and ask little of you beyond the basic conditions it needs to survive. Your little haworthia will grow slowly to reach 4–6 inches tall and similar width, making it a good choice if your sill space is limited. Its low, spiky green-and-white rosettes contrast nicely with upright cacti and succulents that enjoy the same bright, dry environment.

Date I brought you home: _____

What I loved about you from the start: _____

Milestones in your growth: _____

HELP ME GROW

▶ Bright but indirect light will keep your haworthia growing happily. Full sunlight can burn its pretty leaves, especially if it is moved abruptly from indoor lighting to direct sun exposure.

▶ Your haworthia will be cozy in average to warm room temperatures (70–80°F) for most of the year, and it neither wants nor needs the kind of humid environment preferred by many other houseplants. In winter, haworthia appreciates a rest period in cool (60°F) conditions.

▶ A small container filled with a well-drained potting mix, such as one used for cacti, is all your little haworthia needs. Repot your haworthia in spring every year or two to refresh its potting mix. A layer of coarse sand on top of its container will help keep moisture from collecting at the base of its rosette.

FEED ME

▶ From spring through early fall, water your haworthia when the top inch of its potting soil is dry. During the winter, water sparingly, just enough to keep its container from drying out completely. Avoid pouring water into your haworthia's rosette when you give it a drink.

▶ Dilute balanced liquid houseplant fertilizer to half strength and feed your haworthia monthly during the spring and summer. Suspend feedings during its winter rest period.

LOVE ME

Good at sharing: Small size and slow growth make haworthias agreeable pot mates for other succulents or cacti that like the same conditions. Create an attractive, easy-care display in a sandy dish garden with a spiky haworthia and a couple of rounded cacti or smooth-leaved succulents. There are also many forms of haworthias to be found, with different leaf colors and patterns and growth habits. A grouping of different forms of these pleasingly petite succulents offers relatively carefree visual variety.

More, please: With time, your happy haworthia may produce "pups," offsets that form at the base of the main rosette. When repotting in spring, separate these new plants from their parent and pot up your grand-haworthias in their own containers.

Inch plant
(Tradescantia zebrina, Tradescantia albiflora)

Silver- and green-striped leaves with purple undersides and agreeably easy
care requirements make an inch plant a fine adoptee for a casual plant parent
who wants a little color in their life. Dubbed "inch plant" for its speedy growth,
this stripy sprout will quickly fill a hanging basket with its lovely, leafy, slightly
zigzagging stems. A close relative, *Tradescantia fluminensis* has varieties with
green-and-white-striped and pink-, green-, and white-striped foliage. Whatever
the color scheme, one of these tradescantias will reward even modest care
with abundant colorful leaves and occasional tiny pink or white flowers.

Date I brought you home: _____

What I loved about you from the start: _____

Milestones in your growth: _____

HELP ME GROW

▶ Bright to moderate lighting will meet your inch plant's needs year round, and it will even enjoy a bit of direct sunlight, especially if it has prettily variegated leaves.

BETTER WHERE IT'S BRIGHT: Your tradescantia won't do well in constant, blazing sun, but it will be happier in bright conditions than in dim ones. In less-than-bright lighting, inch plant tends to lose its lower leaves and its stems become leggy and bare. Foliage colors become less vibrant in low light, too.

▶ Average household temperatures (60–75°F) will suit your inch plant nicely. Tradescantias are more tolerant of low humidity than many houseplants but they appreciate a bit of additional moisture in the air to relieve the dry conditions caused by winter heating.

▶ Settle your tradescantia into a soil-based potting mix with good drainage. This pretty foliage plant will drape its leafy limbs happily from a hanging basket. Repot every 2–3 years or as needed to relieve crowded roots.

FEED ME

▶ Water to maintain even soil moisture but don't let your inch plant's pot get soggy. Let the top half inch of the potting soil dry out between waterings. Water less frequently in winter, but don't let things dry out completely. Pay attention to signs such as browning leaf tips that indicate the air is too dry.

▶ Serve your inch plant monthly meals of a balanced liquid houseplant fertilizer from spring into early fall. Pause fertilizing during the winter when its growth will slow in response to lower light levels. Overfeeding can cause tradescantia's foliage color to fade.

LOVE ME

Curb my enthusiasm: Prune stems to keep tradescantia's trailing habits in check and encourage bushy, full behavior. Even with regular pruning, your inch plant will tend to lose lower leaves and become more sprawling with age. Rather than fight against this tendency, it's simpler to root cuttings for a new plant and surrender the old, leggy one.

More, please: Cuttings taken from the tips of your inch plant's trailing stems will root easily in water or in moist potting soil. Snip off 3-inch tip cuttings; these will root rather easily at their nodes and you'll have new inch plants to love before you know it. If you root the cuttings in water, transfer them to soil when the new roots reach 1 inch long.

Jade plant

(Crassula ovata)

Shaped like a little tree bearing a crown of smooth, spoon-shaped, rich green leaves, jade plant is considered to bring good fortune to homes where it resides. It's certainly easy to feel lucky when you share the easy-care company of this attractive succulent. Gradually, a jade plant may grow to 2 feet tall with a similar spread. Jades that reach the advanced age of 10 years may bloom in winter if encouraged with a cool rest period. As it grows, your jade plant's spreading crown of fleshy leaves and stems can become top-heavy. Give it a sturdy container to balance the weight and reduce the risk of tipping.

Date I brought you home: _____

What I loved about you from the start: _____

Milestones in your growth: _____

HELP ME GROW

▶ Bright light will help keep your jade plant sturdy and stocky. It will prosper with a few hours each day in full sun, filtered through a sheer curtain or dappled by tree leaves or blinds. Summer outdoors is nice for a jade plant; choose a bright spot out of direct sun.

SIGNS I NEED MORE: If it's not getting enough light, little jade will grow spindly as it stretches and leans toward the light.

COLOR ME HAPPY: In bright sunlight, your jade plant's leaves may develop reddish tints.

▶ Average household temperatures (60–80°F) and average humidity meet jade plant's needs year-round. A cool rest period (55–60°F) in winter may prompt mature plants to produce clusters of starry pink or white flowers.

▶ A sandy potting mix meant for cacti and succulents will provide the drainage your jade plant desires. Repot annually in spring, handling the stems carefully.

FEED ME

▶ Let the top inch of soil dry out between drinks during the spring, summer, and fall. In winter, water just enough to prevent the soil from drying out completely, watching for shriveling leaves that indicate a need for more moisture.

▶ Your jade plant is a light eater. Serve it a balanced fertilizer mixed at half strength two or three times over the course of the spring and summer and pause feedings in the winter.

LOVE ME

Don't let the dust settle: Gently wipe jade plant's smooth foliage with a damp cloth to remove dust and debris that can reduce light absorption. Work gently to avoid breaking the fleshy leaves and stems.

Crowd control: You may find that the jade "plant" you brought home from the store is a group of multiple plants grown in a single pot to create a bushy effect. To enjoy your jade plant's true form, give each plant in the pot its own container and enjoy a small collection of pretty jade trees.

More, please: Like many succulents, your jade plant's leaves can be rooted in moistened, sandy potting mix with relative ease. Taking 3-inch cuttings from branch tips for rooting results in a bigger sprout for your effort. Either way, let leaf or tip cuttings dry for at least 24 hours before "planting" them in a container to root. Wear gloves when taking cuttings to protect your skin from contact with irritating sap, and place your pretty little tree where it's out of the reach of curious pets or kids.

Kalanchoes

(Kalanchoe species and hybrids)

Don't let uncertainty over pronouncing the name (ka-luhn-KO-ee) of this quirky group of succulents keep you from bringing home one (or more!). Perhaps the best known are the hybrids of *Kalanchoe blossfeldiana*, sometimes called flaming Katy, bright bloomers that carry clusters of star-shaped red, orange, pink, yellow, or white flowers. Often sold among outdoor annuals in the spring and summer or as flowering houseplants around the winter holidays, kalanchoes bloom for nearly 2 months but have very specific requirements to get them to repeat their floral performance. Other species, such as devil's backbone and panda plant, may catch your eye with their unique and attractive foliage; *Kalanchoe pumila* is a pink-flowering species with spoon-shaped, fleshy gray-green leaves that have a powdery white coating.

Date I brought you home: _____

What I loved about you from the start: _____

Milestones in your growth: _____

HELP ME GROW

▶ Your kalanchoe will enjoy full sun on your windowsill. If it's summering outdoors, a spot with filtered sun or shade is best. In bright sun, its leaves may redden around the edges, but too much sun can cause brown splotches.

▶ During the spring and summer, kalanchoe likes things on the warm side (70–85°F), while cooler temperatures (55–70°F) please it in fall and winter. Its succulent nature lets it tolerate dry indoor air better than many houseplants do.

▶ Potting soil amended with perlite or coarse sand or a mix labeled for cacti and succulents will provide the drainage your kalanchoe desires. Repot yearly in spring or start fresh with cuttings of a plant that is more than 2 years old.

FEED ME

▶ Water your kalanchoe from the bottom to avoid wetting its leaves and creating conditions that favor rotting foliage and stems. Keep the soil evenly moist during the spring and summer, letting the top inch dry out between drinks. In fall and winter, water occasionally and lightly, just enough to keep the soil from drying out.

▶ Monthly servings of a balanced fertilizer from late spring into late fall will support your kalanchoe's good health. Pause feedings in winter into early spring.

LOVE ME

Bring back the blooms: Coaxing your kalanchoe back into bloom isn't impossible, but it requires parental discipline regarding bedtime. Start by giving your baby the benefit of long, sunny days outdoors during the summer. When the weather turns chilly, bring your kalanchoe indoors to a cool, bright location where you can keep it in total darkness for 14 hours every night for 2–4 weeks. This process should prompt your sprout to produce buds and blooms in about 6–8 weeks.

Lots of little ones: If you've always dreamed of having a large family, but lack lots of space, the plant known variously as devil's backbone, alligator plant, and mother-of-thousands (*Kalanchoe daigremontiana*) is perfect for you. From a rosette of short-stemmed, lance-shaped foliage, this plant will deliver countless baby plants that form continuously along the edges of its toothed leaves. The babies, known as adventitious plantlets, drop from the parent plant onto soil below and grow into their own leaf-baby-sprouting machine. In climates where it can live outdoors, devil's backbone is considered an invasive nuisance, but it can be a charming and prolific novelty in your home, where its reproductive tendencies make it a conversation piece rather than a pest.

Money tree
(Pachira aquatica)

If your favorite dad line is "money doesn't grow on trees," you might appreciate adopting a money tree. With glossy leaflets that fan out in a palm-shaped arrangement above stems that are traditionally braided together, the money tree is considered a symbol of financial luck in many Asian countries. Your own money tree may or may not enhance your bank account, but it can grow to be a statuesque family member that will make you feel lucky by looking great with a modest amount of care.

Date I brought you home: _____

What I loved about you from the start: _____

Milestones in your growth: _____

HELP ME GROW

▶ Place your tree where it will enjoy plenty of bright but indirect light, such as near a south- or east-facing window.

LIGHT ALTERNATIVES: Your money tree will tolerate life under fluorescent lighting. It can also spend the summer months outdoors, where it will do best in filtered sunlight conditions. Make moves from bright to shaded or indoors to outdoors gradually to avoid sending your money tree into a leaf-dropping funk or risking sunburn on its pretty leaves.

▶ Keep your money tree cozy with normal room temperatures (60–75°F) and add a bit of humidity with a pebble tray and/or occasional misting. Cooler temperatures are okay during the winter months when growth slows, but conditions below 55°F may give your money tree an unwelcome chill.

▶ A soil-based potting mix with perlite and/or coarse sand for improved drainage will satisfy your money plant's needs for moisture and adequate aeration around its roots. Repot if the roots become crowded in the container but don't be quick to move baby money plant into a big-kid container. Keeping the roots snug is what keeps your money tree from growing too large for indoor spaces, plus large pots increase the risk of soggy soil and resulting root rot.

FEED ME

▶ Even soil moisture and good drainage are best for your money tree's health. Let the top half inch of the potting soil dry out between waterings. Cut back on drinks during the fall and winter when your money tree will take a rest but keep things humid during nap time.

▶ In nature, money trees grow quite large, and too much fertilizing will bring out a tendency to stretch. Serve your tree houseplant fertilizer once per month in spring and summer and every other month in fall and winter.

LOVE ME

Mini money trees: The same easygoing nature that allows money trees to be braided also makes them good subjects for bonsai.

Parental controls: Once your money tree reaches the height and pot size that fit your family plan, provide appropriate limits to keep it from growing out of hand. Instead of moving it into larger pots, refresh the potting mix on top of the container every year or two, and pinch back stem tips to control size and encourage branching and sturdy growth. Pinching shoots and pruning the roots when you repot should be done in the spring when your money tree is resuming active growth after a winter rest.

Monstera, Swiss cheese plant

(Monstera deliciosa)

Even if you start with a little monstera, be prepared to make lots of room for this vigorous jungle climber. From a modest sprout with glossy leaves, your monstera will climb over time to a height of 6 feet or more (with proper support). Its heart-shaped leaves will reach or exceed 12 inches across, and mature foliage will develop the deeply cut lobes and dramatic holes, or windows, that earn monstera nicknames such as "Swiss cheese plant" and "split-leaf philodendron." Fill a bright open space with a dramatic monstera and enjoy its large personality.

Date I brought you home:_____

What I loved about you from the start:_____

Milestones in your growth:_____

HELP ME GROW

▶ Bright, filtered or indirect light will keep your little monstera growing, green, and gorgeous. Full summer sun is too much for its broad leaves but it will enjoy a few hours of direct sun in the winter.

BRIGHTEN MY DAYS: While this climber will tolerate moderate lighting, it will demonstrate its desire for more sun by producing fewer, smaller, and less-holey leaves on elongated, spindly stalks.

▶ Your monstera will be comfortable in normal to warm room temperatures (65–80°F) and will appreciate added humidity when the air around it is warmer than 70–75°F. Give it a tray of moist pebbles and occasional misting to prevent its leaves from drying out in arid indoor air.

▶ Snuggle monstera's roots in a soil-based potting mix balanced with peat moss or leaf mold and sand. Repot every 2–3 years until you reach the maximum sustainable pot size for your space; refresh the top layer of the potting soil annually thereafter.

TUCK ME IN: As it grows, your monstera will produce pencil-diameter aerial roots. In its natural habitat, these help it collect moisture from the air and anchor it to the trees it clambers over. Provide baby with a roomy pot and guide aerial roots near its base into the potting soil.

FEED ME

▶ Allow the top inch of your monstera's potting soil to dry out between drinks during spring and summer; reduce watering somewhat in the winter months when its growth will be slower, but watch for signs it is too dry or suffering from low humidity.

▶ Serve your monstera a balanced fertilizer every 2–3 weeks from spring into early fall. In the winter, fertilize once a month.

LOVE ME

Give me a boost: Provide a sturdy moss-covered climbing post to mimic the trees monstera clambers up in its natural environment. Gently tie stems to the post as your monstera stretches upward and guide aerial roots into the moss.

Polish, please: Wipe your monstera's glossy leaves regularly with a damp cloth to remove dust and keep them looking their best.

Don't eat this cheese: Although this monstera is called "deliciosa," that only applies to the fruit produced by mature plants growing outdoors; indoor monsteras are unlikely to bloom and form fruits. The rest of the plant is toxic and not at all Swiss cheese–like. Keep pets and people from nibbling!

Moth orchids

(Phalaenopsis species and hybrids)

Sprays of long-lasting flowers that hover on arching stems over low, broad leaves give moth orchids a charm that tempts prospective plant parents to adopt one of these beauties on the spot. The good news for captivated moms and dads is that these orchids are among the most accepting of life in average household conditions. If you meet its rather reasonable requirements, your moth orchid will delight you with an annual display of elegant flowers for 6 or more weeks in the spring.

Date I brought you home: _____

What I loved about you from the start: _____

Milestones in your growth: _____

HELP ME GROW

▶ This moth is drawn to bright, indirect or filtered light, and is more tolerant than other orchids of moderate lighting, although too little light will reduce its chances of blooming.

▶ Your moth orchid will exist happily in temperatures of 65–80°F year-round. A cool "vacation" in 55–60°F temperatures for 2–3 weeks in winter can help stimulate flower formation.

UPS AND DOWNS: If you're in the habit of turning down the thermostat at night and back up in the daytime, your moth orchid will approve. Within its preferred temperature range, it will be happiest if it enjoys cooler nights and warmer days.

▶ Plant this baby in a bark-based orchid potting mix. Avoid covering the aerial roots resting on top. Repot every 2 years as its bark mix starts to deteriorate, gently separating the roots from the old mix and examining them before repotting. Healthy roots are silvery green; trim off any that are dried out or dark and mushy.

FEED ME

▶ Tap water may displease this pretty baby. Water it with filtered or distilled water at room temperature, taking care to avoid wetting the foliage. Watering by setting the pot in a container of tepid water for 10–15 minutes and then letting it drain is a good technique; do this in the morning once every week or so during the spring and summer, allowing the top inch of the growing medium to dry out in between drinks. Water less during the winter.

DON'T SPILL ON ME: Your moth orchid may pout if you let moisture linger on its leaves. Black spots on foliage, indicating fungal infection, are a result of letting water remain on the leaves for too long.

▶ Every 2–3 weeks throughout spring and summer, serve a balanced fertilizer diluted to half strength. Fertilize monthly during the fall and winter.

LOVE ME

Bring on more blooms: When the flowers fade from your moth orchid's spray, snip the flower stem back to just above a bump or node to stimulate production of another spray of blooms.

Read my leaves: Your moth orchid's medium-green, broad, somewhat fleshy, floppy leaves can tell you a lot about its mood. Young leaves that are yellow or pale may point to a need for more fertilizing or too much sun exposure; very dark green leaves point to too little light. While wilting can indicate a need for watering, leaves that do not recover after a drink may mean a problem at the roots that's preventing water uptake. And limp, lax leaves may be telling you the air is too dry.

Nerve plant
(Fittonia verschaffeltii)

The eye-catching vein-laced leaves of nerve plant fairly scream "take me home with you" to would-be plant parents. These pretty rainforest natives produce low, spreading mounds of 1- to 2-inch-long rich green leaves overlaid with a vivid netting of veins in pink, white, or green. Although the name "nerve plant" refers to its showy vein display, your fittonia can be a bit nervous about its growing conditions and is quick to show its displeasure when things are not just right. Humidity keeps nerve plant happy and this baby is the perfect choice for adding pizzazz to a moist terrarium.

Date I brought you home: _____

What I loved about you from the start: _____

Milestones in your growth: _____

HELP ME GROW

▶ Bright to moderate, indirect light will satisfy your nerve plant and it doesn't mind living in the glow of a fluorescent light, but it can't tolerate direct sun.

▶ Nerve plant likes normal room temperatures (65–80°F) and high humidity. Dry air is its nemesis and will cause its pretty leaves to develop icky brown tips.

▶ Nestle your nerve plant in a moisture-retentive potting mix. Plant in a terrarium or dish garden, where you can easily give it the humid conditions it needs. Repot in spring every year or two.

FEED ME

▶ Water your nerve plant regularly with tepid water to maintain evenly moist soil conditions but keep an eye on drainage. Consistent parenting is necessary to get nerve plant's watering just right, but it's worth it for this adorable baby's mesmerizing veined leaves.

INCLINED TO DRAMA: Pay careful attention to your nerve plant's watering needs to avoid its dramatic response to soil that is too dry or too wet. A nerve plant that dries out will literally collapse and, depending on how dry things have become, may not perk up again. Yellowing leaves are a sign that things are too soggy for your nerve plant's tastes.

▶ Fortunately, nerve plant is not a picky eater. Serve it a balanced plant food on a monthly schedule during the spring and summer; space feedings out to every 6–8 weeks from fall through winter.

LOVE ME

Pinch me: Nerve plant grows to just 4–6 inches tall with a spread of about 12 inches, depending on the variety. A happy nerve plant may grow a bit sprawling in its joy and need a parent's hand to rein it in. If your nerve plant's new growth begins to tend toward vining, pinch branch tips back to a pair of leaves to encourage bushier behavior. You'll also want to pinch off any flower spikes that appear in summer; your nerve plant's glory is its handsome foliage.

More, please: Stem tip cuttings with three or four leaf pairs will root easily in moist potting soil and warm, humid conditions.

Norfolk Island pine
(Araucaria heterophylla)

Few houseplants are more enchanting than a petite Norfolk Island pine all dressed up for the holidays like an apartment-scale Tannenbaum. But there's more to this pretty conifer than festive décor. Growing slowly to about 6 feet tall, this charming little tree holds its needle-clad branches in horizontal layers that give it an architectural presence. While its size makes it a focal point, its texture is almost feathery, and it contrasts nicely with plants that have rounded, glossy leaves. In the right spot in your home, your little Norfolk pine can be a long-lived member of the family, and you'll find its quiet beauty makes it easy to love.

Date I brought you home: _____

What I loved about you from the start: _____

Milestones in your growth: _____

HELP ME GROW

▶ Bright light is best for the good health of your Norfolk pine and it will be at its best with a couple hours of direct sun each day. A spot near a south or west window will make it very happy. In too little light, your pine's branches will droop and shed their needles.

GIVE IT A TWIRL: Turn your Norfolk pine's pot by a quarter turn each week to balance light exposure.

▶ As befits a plant associated with the winter holidays, Norfolk pine enjoys life on the cool side of household temperatures (55–75°F). As the air around it gets warmer, your Norfolk pine's need for humidity will increase. Mist its branches regularly during the winter when indoor heating can stress it out. For this statuesque plant, a humidifier might be a worthy accessory.

▶ Fill your Norfolk pine's pot with a soil-based potting medium with coarse sand for improved drainage. A layer of gravel in the bottom of its pot will also contribute to good drainage and will add stabilizing weight. Repot annually in the spring, treating the rather sparse and delicate roots carefully to avoid damaging them. Wear gloves when repotting to protect your hands from the prickly needles that clothe your pine's main stem as well as its branches.

FEED ME

▶ Year-round, water often to maintain lightly moist soil in your pine's pot. In winter, pay close attention to soil moisture as well as humidity, particularly if direct sun shines on your pine and warms things up around it.

NO FAN OF EXTREMES: Neither dry soil nor soggy conditions will please your Norfolk pine, and problems in the pot will inevitably cause it to shed needles and entire branches that will never grow back.

▶ From spring into early fall, feed your pretty pine with a balanced fertilizer once a month. A couple of times a year, treat it to a foliar fertilizer spray to give it a nutrient boost straight to its foliage.

LOVE ME

Don't prune me: A slow grower, your Norfolk pine doesn't need you to prune its branches. As it grows, its lower branches will naturally die and should be removed.

A pine (not) from Down Under: A conifer, but not a true pine, your pretty little tree's ancestors came from Norfolk Island off the coast of Australia. In the wild, these trees may reach nearly 200 feet tall, which is an inspirational story you can share with your sprout on a wintry evening.

Orchids

Orchids have a reputation for being finicky that is somewhat undeserved. Certainly most orchids have very specific requirements for producing their pretty flowers. But from a plant parent's perspective, it's easier to think of your little bloomer as confident, self-aware, and determined to get what it wants. Succeeding as an orchid parent, then, means learning about the needs of your own special orchid baby and doing your best to satisfy those needs. The reward for your efforts is the satisfaction of seeing your little orchid bring forth its remarkable blooms as a result of your loving care.

Date I brought you home: _____

What I loved about you from the start: _____

Milestones in your growth: _____

You are a: _____

HELP ME GROW

▶ Orchids' light needs vary, but most houseplant varieties need bright but indirect light.

▶ There are orchids suited to the full range of "average household temperatures," but most species are happiest in a narrower segment that may be at the cool end of that range, the warm end of it, or right in the middle. Keeping your orchid in a location that matches its preferred temperature profile will benefit its overall health and increase the likelihood of bringing it into bloom.

NIGHT AND DAY: Within its preferred range of temperatures, your orchid will benefit from nighttime temperatures that are on the cool side of its likes and daytime temperatures that are perhaps 15 degrees warmer. A good way to satisfy this need for difference between day and night is to put orchids outdoors for the summer months.

▶ Orchids prefer to rest their roots in a chunky mix composed mostly of bark with a bit of peat or other goodies mixed in. This custom orchid blend lets air flow around the roots and keeps things from becoming soggy, but it loses these important qualities as the bark gradually decomposes. Repot your orchid every 2 years to give it fresh medium to sink its roots into, keeping its pot size on the snug side.

FEED ME

▶ Match your watering to your orchid's needs. Species that form pseudobulbs, swollen stems that store moisture, have different watering needs than terrestrial orchids that may require more water. Epiphytic orchids are accustomed to drying out in between drinks.

WATER WISELY: Overwatering is far more harmful to orchids than underwatering. Tend toward giving your plant less rather than more.

▶ Frequent, light feeding during the active growing season, using a dilute balanced fertilizer or a formula specifically for orchids, is good general advice, but needs vary depending on the species and the time of year. Orchids that enter a rest period in the winter should not be fertilized until new growth resumes.

LOVE ME

CATTLEYA ORCHIDS (*CATTLEYA* SPECIES AND HYBRIDS)

Pin one on: Cattleyas are the orchids most commonly grown for corsages. These epiphytic orchids bloom in late winter and early spring, producing big, frilly flowers. After blooming, cattleyas enter a 6-week rest period, during which they need only enough water to keep their pseudobulbs from shriveling.

Bright lights, big bloomers: A cattleya needs bright light year-round, warm temperatures, and high humidity to bring forth its blooms. Direct sun is a no-no, as are temperatures below 60°F.

DANCING LADY ORCHIDS (*ONCIDIUM* SPECIES AND HYBRIDS)

Fluttering butterflies: The dancing ladies, also interpreted as butterflies, produce stems of multiple small flowers. Oncidiums may bloom in summer, fall, or spring, and some hybrids will bloom twice in a year.

Bright and polite: Dancing lady orchids appreciate bright lighting and cool to moderate temperatures (60–75°F). Tall, branching stems of flowers may require additional parental support in the form of a stake. A sturdy but not overlarge container will prevent your beauty from tipping.

DENDROBIUM ORCHIDS (*DENDROBIUM* SPECIES AND HYBRIDS)

Spray orchids: The spray, or lei, orchids produce stems of multiple flowers that may last for several weeks; some species are fragrant. Most dendrobiums bloom in spring; some will repeat their floral show in late summer.

I need my rest: Most dendrobiums prefer warmth and regular watering and feeding during their active growth period, and a clearly defined winter rest period in cooler conditions and just enough water to keep them from drying out completely.

LADY'S SLIPPER ORCHIDS (*PAPHIOPEDILUM* SPECIES AND HYBRIDS)

If this shoe fits: A pretty orchid with low clusters of solid green or mottled leaves, your paphiopedilum will raise its "slipper" on a tall stalk to bloom for 2 months or longer. Lady's slippers have more modest light requirements than many orchids and will even grow and bloom under fluorescent lighting, but avoid placing in direct sun. Cool nights and warm days keep them comfortable, but they require high humidity in warm conditions. Keep them on a moist pebble tray.

Look at the leaf: Use leaf color as a guide to setting the thermostat. A paphiopedilum with plain green leaves will prefer cooler nights around 60°F and days of 75°F, while one with mottled foliage likes slightly warmer temperatures (65–80°F).

Help me up: A supporting stick fastened to the flower stem before the bud opens may be necessary to keep the blossom from drooping. After flowering is finished, reduce watering without letting the potting mix dry out completely.

Palms

Palms became popular as houseplants in Victorian times, but these ancient, mostly tropical plants remain handsome additions to any home with space and love to spare. A palm species that grows large in an outdoor setting may remain at more manageable heights when constrained by a pot, but you'll want to make sure you have plenty of room if your bouncing baby sprout is a palm with vertical growth potential. Because of the way they grow, pruning back a palm that becomes too tall is not a satisfactory solution, as it can injure or even kill the plant. With room to grow and the conditions and care it craves, your little palm can be part of your family for a very long time.

Date I brought you home: _____

What I loved about you from the start: _____

Milestones in your growth: _____

You are a: _____

HELP ME GROW

▶ Bright light that includes a few hours per day of direct sun will satisfy most palms, but light needs vary by species.

DON'T GO CHANGING: Abrupt changes in lighting can cast your palm into a deep and possibly fatal funk. The palm you bring home is likely an immature plant that would naturally be shaded beneath taller vegetation. It also has been acclimated for life and light indoors and will not be glad to find itself in full sun on a patio. Likewise, a palm that has been growing outdoors will suffer if moved suddenly into dim indoor lighting. Make changes to a palm's position gradually and keep palms that spend summer outside in a shaded location.

▶ Average to very warm household temperatures will keep your palm cozy, and most species are averse to chilly conditions. Below 60–65°F, your palm's already slow growth rate will slow even more. More tolerant of dry air than many houseplants, palms benefit from having moisture added to the air via a pebble tray and/or occasional misting with tepid water. Brown leaf tips may be a sign that things are too dry for your palm's liking.

▶ While not every palm species hails from a desert island like in the comics, most enjoy the superior drainage conditions of a sandy potting mix. A layer of gravel in the bottom of the pot and potting medium composed of soil, leaf mold, peat, and sand will work for most palms. Snug pots help control the size of palms growing indoors; repot only every 3 years or as needed when roots are crowded. Handle the thick, fleshy roots carefully to avoid damage. Always replant your palm at the same depth when repotting and tap the container firmly to settle the potting mix around the roots. Use a sturdy container to balance tall palms and prevent tipping.

FEED ME

▶ Your palm may be a bit picky about its water and will be happiest if you give it drinks of distilled or filtered water or rainwater. Watering needs vary by species, but most enjoy lightly moist soil during the spring and summer months and reduced watering in fall and winter, when growth typically slows.

▶ Most palms have modest feeding needs that are best met with a spring serving of slow-release fertilizer and occasional additions of compost to the surface of their potting mix. Too much fertilizer can cause salts to accumulate in the potting soil and injure your palm's roots. Flushing out excess salts by flooding the soil with water, letting it drain, and then repeating that process is beneficial a couple of times per year.

LOVE ME ♥

FAN PALM (*CHAMAEROPS HUMILIS*)

Your #1 fan: A sun-loving palm that enjoys warm, bright days and cool nights, a fan palm produces broad fronds fringed with lancelike leaf tips that fan out to as much as 2 feet across. This palm grows slowly to reach a mature height of about 4 feet and can easily spread as wide. Keep your fan palm happy in a spot where it gets direct sun for 3–4 hours each day. An occasional tepid shower will help to clean the surface of your fan palm's dramatic, broad fronds.

More, please: Fan palms form suckers (new plants) at their base. When a sucker reaches 8–10 inches tall, it can be carefully separated from the parent plant and planted in a pot of its own. With time, you can grow your own fan club!

FEATHER PALM (*CHRYSALIDOCARPUS LUTESCENS*)

Airy and elegant: The arching and many-leaved fronds of this palm resemble tall feathers with yellow-orange stems. Also called areca palm and butterfly palm, this graceful plant likes a spot in bright but indirect or filtered light. This feathery friend prefers warmth and dislikes temperatures below 55–60°F. A slow grower, your feather palm will reach 6–7 feet over time. As a feather palm ages,

an older stem or two will naturally yellow and die every year; clip these off at the base to keep your palm tidy.

Summer outside: Your feather palm can benefit from spending summer outdoors in a bright but shaded location. When it's time to return indoors, inspect your pretty feather palm carefully for hidden hitchhiking pests that may have tucked in among the fronds. Palms of all sorts are particularly prone to scale insects, and these sneaky, armored pests can make a palm sickly and sad before you realize they are there. Look for raised brown bumps on the undersides of fronds; sticky, shiny, drippy leaves are another sign of scale activity. Carefully scrape off the bumps, which are scale insects covered by a waxy shell. Follow removal with insecticidal soap spray (test on a leaf to make sure your palm will tolerate this) and repeat inspection and treatment until things are under control.

FISHTAIL PALM (*CARYOTA MITIS*)

Casual elegance: Fishtail palm's triangle-shaped fronds have irregular edges that give it a rakish air. This palm's stems grow upright in a gently arching vase shape to slowly reach 8 feet tall. Place your fishtail palm in bright, filtered sunlight in a warm room—it will not appreciate temperatures below 55°F. Pay attention to its humidity needs with a pebble tray and water to maintain light, even soil moisture without soggy soil.

Shower me: Dry, warm indoor air can make your fishtail palm a target for spider mites, which thrive in such conditions. Give baby a refreshing lukewarm shower a couple of times per year to rinse away any pests and dust on the leaves and boost humidity to keep its fronds comfortable. Brown leaf tips are a sign that the air is too dry, but an entire frond that turns yellow and drops off is normal on an occasional (yearly) basis.

KENTIA PALM (*HOWEA FORSTERIANA*)

A palm with potential: The loose fans of kentia palm's glossy, dark green leaves can reach to heights of 8 feet or more, but this handsome upright palm grows so slowly that it may be many years before its fronds brush your ceiling. Kentia palm likes bright, indirect light but tolerates lower lighting. In modest light exposures, your kentia palm will increase very slowly. Pale foliage accompanied by listless growth may indicate that things are too dim; provide supplemental lighting or move your kentia closer to a bright window.

Glad to stay put: Kentia palms prefer to fit snugly in the pot and are not keen about having their rather fragile roots disturbed. Repot your little kentia only when its roots become quite crowded in the container, handling very gently and increasing pot size only modestly.

LADY PALM (*RHAPIS EXCELSA*)

Lady's fingers: Also called bamboo palm, this congenial lady bears dark green fronds made up of five to nine leaflets that fan out like fingers at the end of 9- to 12-inch leaf stalks. Kept slightly root-bound indoors in bright, filtered light, your lady palm will slowly grow to no more than 5 feet tall.

Nice and easy: Lady palm tolerates lower lighting than many other palms and prefers indirect light to full sun, which can cause its leaves to turn yellowish. Your lady enjoys a modest diet, too, and will be happy with a bit of slow-release fertilizer in its pot in the spring. Mist her leaves in the summer or when indoor heating makes things dry to keep the leaflet tips from browning and reduce the risk of spider mite woes. Like most palms, lady palm prefers to drink rainwater or filtered water and will fuss if served softened or fluoridated drinks. Flush her pot once or twice a year to keep fertilizer salts from building up, and repot in a sandy soil mix every couple of years until your lady palm reaches the size that's right for your space.

PARLOR PALM (*CHAMAEDOREA ELEGANS*)

Fancy and feathery: The elegant leaflets of this petite palm have graced the parlors of society since the Victorian era. If limited space and lighting in your home make it difficult to accommodate larger palms, a pretty parlor palm can class up your place and is small enough to sit on a table in moderate to bright, indirect light. Avoid placing your parlor palm in direct sun, which can turn its leaf tips brown; it will grow under fluorescent lights if a window isn't available.

Favored for freshening: Because it can be happy under fluorescent lighting, parlor palm is popular as an office plant and it offers the added benefit of helping to clear the air in places where it grows. It doesn't mind dry conditions but will benefit from a pebble tray or misting to keep its lovely fronds from drying out.

Your parlor palm needs lightly moist soil but will suffer if its pot is too soggy.

Good grooming: As your parlor palm ages, some of its fronds will naturally die off and should be trimmed off at the base. If its leaflets are a less than healthy dark green, offer it a dilute solution of balanced houseplant fertilizer in summer to supplement its diet. Occasionally wiping its foliage with a damp cloth (or giving it a rinse under a tepid shower) will remove dust that can keep your palm from getting enough light and allows you to inspect for spider mites before they cause serious damage.

Fan palm

Peace lilies

(Spathiphyllum species)

Refined good looks and modest care requirements have earned spathiphyllums, commonly known as peace lilies or spaths, a place in malls, offices, and other commercial settings around the globe. For plant parents in need of a confidence boost or those who are looking for a sprout that can make the best of a low-light location, a peace lily will respond to your loving care with a fountain of glossy green leaves and long-lasting white tear-drop-shaped spathes, each clasped around a creamy yellow flower stalk. Varieties range from towering 6-footers to petite selections that may grow no more than 12 inches tall.

Date I brought you home: _____

What I loved about you from the start: _____

Milestones in your growth: _____

HELP ME GROW

▶ Adaptability to a range of lighting conditions has contributed to peace lily's popularity; it will get along under artificial lights and in moderate natural lighting, as from a north-facing window. Your own pretty peace lily will be happier, though, if it receives moderate to bright, indirect light, at least in spring and summer when it is actively growing.

SUNSCREEN, PLEASE: Peace lily may develop brown, dried patches on its foliage in response to too much direct sun.

▶ Average to warm room temperatures (60–85°F) will keep your peace lily cozy; guard it from drafts or temperatures below 55°F. Give it a pebble tray and occasional misting to maintain humidity in warm, indoor air.

▶ Peace lily is not picky but will appreciate a loose and well-drained mix in a pot that's on the snug side. Repot in spring to freshen up its potting medium.

FEED ME

▶ Water your peace lily when the top half inch of its potting soil has dried out. Evenly, lightly moist soil throughout spring and summer will keep your spath happy. In winter, water less frequently, but don't let the soil dry out completely.

I WILT AND I WILT NOT: Your peace lily will signal extreme thirst by drooping dramatically and will recover equally dramatically when you supply it with water. But repeated wilting is tough on any plant.

▶ Feed your peace lily every 2–3 weeks from spring through fall with a balanced houseplant fertilizer diluted to half strength. Reduce feedings to once per month in winter.

LOVE ME

Spaths in space: NASA has named spathiphyllum one of the best houseplants for purifying the air indoors, recognizing its ability to remove formaldehyde and other nasty pollutants from its surroundings.

Perfectly polished: Give your baby a warm shower once in a while to freshen its foliage and, in between showers, gently wipe leaves clean with a damp cloth.

More, please: A peace lily that wilts often in spite of appropriate watering may be telling you its roots are too crowded. Divide very pot-bound plants in spring, carefully separating clumps of leaves attached to shallow rhizomes. Replant at the same depth in fresh potting soil. Let divisions settle in for 2–3 months before fertilizing.

Peperomias

(Peperomia species)

Peperomias include several popular houseplants grown for their colorful, sometimes fleshy, textured, or metallic-finished foliage and unusual snaky flower spikes. Most are low-growing, ranging from 6–12 inches tall, and hold their attractive leaves and narrow creamy flower heads on stalks that may be pink or red. Once you get to know one of these adorable little plants, you'll want to adopt several so you can enjoy the full range of wonderfully varied foliage effects that peperomias have to offer. Although their looks may vary, a collection of peperomias makes a colorful display of plants that enjoy the same general care requirements.

Date I brought you home: _____

What I loved about you from the start: _____

Milestones in your growth: _____

HELP ME GROW

▶ Choose lighting based on your peperomia's foliage—moderate to bright, indirect lighting suits most types, but those with variegated foliage benefit from a bit more sun to help maintain their colors. These pretty plants will also grow happily under bright fluorescent lighting.

▶ Average warm room temperatures of 65–75°F are comfortable for peperomias. To satisfy the humidity needs of these rainforest plants, place a moist pebble tray under your peperomia's pot. Skip the mister—it dislikes water on its foliage.

▶ Nestle your peperomia's roots in a light and airy potting mix that includes peat and perlite for superior drainage. Repot in spring every 2–3 years to give it fresh potting mix but keep your baby in a small pot to help reduce the risk of overwatering. A low, shallow pot is a good choice.

FEED ME

▶ Water when the top half inch of the potting soil is dry, using lukewarm water and avoiding the leaves. Reduce watering in winter when lower light causes growth to slow, but avoid a complete dry-out. Thin, transparent-looking foliage is an indication that baby is thirsty.

I FRET WHEN TOO WET: Plants getting too much to drink may drop their pretty leaves or collapse in a funk. A plant that is wilting despite regular watering may have developed root rot.

▶ Peperomia is a light eater. Serve it a balanced fertilizer diluted to half the recommended strength every 3–4 weeks from spring into fall. Feed every 6 weeks during the winter.

LOVE ME

Watermelons, radiators, and (baby) rubber plants: Popular peperomias include watermelon peperomia (*Peperomia argyreia*), which has smooth, round, broadly pointed leaves striped in silver and green atop reddish stems, and radiator plant (*Peperomia caperata*), a 6- to 8-inch-tall mound of heart-shaped deeply ridged foliage that may be reddish, deep green, or silvery with contrasting veins. Baby rubber plant (*Peperomia obtusifolia*) grows more upright than its kin and has elongated oval leaves that look like smaller versions of the foliage of *Ficus elastica*. Depending on the variety, baby rubber plant may have red-tinted deep green leaves or green leaves with white-and-yellow variegation.

More, please: Cut off a young, healthy leaf with an inch of stem and "plant" it in lightly moist potting soil. Water sparingly until rooting occurs.

Philodendrons

(Philodendron species)

Philodendrons are so agreeable, adaptable, and attractive that it's easy to see why they are among the most popular and widely grown houseplants. Their glossy, often heart-shaped leaves make them easy to love, whether they are vining or clump-forming. Your own little phil' may sport colorful or variegated leaves as it climbs (under your guidance) or dangles from a hanging basket, or it might be your best office buddy and grow happily by your side beneath fluorescent lights. Keep your philodendron out of the reach of curious pets and toddlers, as its toxic parts are not for tasting.

Date I brought you home: _____

What I loved about you from the start: _____

Milestones in your growth: _____

You are a: _____

HELP ME GROW

▶ Moderate to bright, indirect light satisfies most types of philodendrons.

BOOST MY EXPOSURE: Philodendrons' popularity as houseplants is owed in part to their tolerance of modest light conditions. Even so, your own dear philodendron will benefit from time spent in bright, indirect light during the spring and summer when it's actively growing, and it won't fuss about being moved in order to soak up some additional (filtered) rays.

▶ Philodendrons are comfortable in average to warm household temperatures, and may sulk if things get too chilly (below 60°F). Your philodendron will thank you for a pebble tray or other means of increasing humidity around its leaves during the winter when heating makes indoor air uncomfortably dry.

▶ Snuggle a philodendron's roots in a peat-based potting mix that drains well. Repot every year or two, keeping the roots somewhat snug in their container and increasing pot size only when the roots fill their pot.

FEED ME

▶ Water to maintain evenly, lightly moist soil through spring and summer and into the fall. Let the top of the mix dry out between waterings and avoid soggy conditions. In winter, reduce watering, providing just enough to prevent the soil from drying out completely.

▶ Leafy philodendrons appreciate the nitrogen boost of a fertilizer for foliage plants. Serve up monthly from spring into early fall; decrease feedings to every 6 weeks during winter.

LOVE ME

BIRD'S NEST PHILODENDRONS (*PHILODENDRON* HYBRIDS)

Nesting spot: Producing a cluster of large, broadly lance-shaped leaves held upright on sturdy stalks, bird's nest philodendrons are non-climbing hybrids that often feature colorful foliage and/or leaf stems. Your bird's nest philodendron will grow happily under bright fluorescent lights and can be an attractive and easy-care office companion.

Good grooming: Wipe your sprout's broad foliage occasionally with a damp cloth to keep it glossy and free of dust that will interfere with light absorption. A pebble tray or humidifier to protect against dry indoor air helps maintain this plant's handsome looks.

BLUSHING PHILODENDRON (*PHILODENDRON ERUBESCENS*)

I'm blushing: Arrowhead-shaped leaves with coppery red undersides adorn reddish-purple stems that vine and climb with proper parental guidance. Don't be embarrassed to give it your support, helping it climb up a bark- or moss-covered post by fastening its vines with pins or twist ties. Gradually those stems will produce aerial roots that take hold of the support and you can remove the temporary fasteners.

Rinse and repeat: An occasional lukewarm shower will help to clean off dust from your blushing philodendron's broad leaves, which may reach 10 inches long and 7 inches across as the plant matures. In between showers, wipe leaves occasionally with a damp cloth. Mist the supporting pole to give aerial roots a refreshing drink, especially in winter when the added humidity will be welcomed.

HEARTLEAF PHILODENDRON (*PHILODENDRON SCANDENS*)

Easy to love: An agreeable vine clad in glossy, deep green, heart-shaped leaves, this philodendron will grow happily in your home and your heart with its easygoing ways. Your heartleaf philodendron can trail from a hanging basket or a planter placed atop a shelf, or you can teach it to climb up a support. Pinch back the stem tips to encourage your little phil' to produce more leafy stems.

Help me grow up: Guide your heartleaf philodendron in its climb up a moss-covered post, using twist ties or florist's tape to fasten its vining stem where you want it to grow. With time, aerial roots will form and baby will hold on by itself, and you can proudly remove the "training wheels."

More, please: If your heartleaf philodendron gets too long and sprawling for your home, it can be easily propagated by taking cuttings from the tips of its stems and rooting them using those same aerial roots that help it climb. Take a 3- to 4-inch segment from the tip of a vine, cutting just below a leaf. Remove all but a leaf or two and tuck the cutting into moistened seed-starting medium in a small pot. Cover the container with a plastic bag to maintain humidity, and place out of direct sun. Mist as needed to keep suitably moist and watch for new growth that indicates roots have formed.

Piggyback plant, mother-of-thousands
(Tolmiea menziesii)

There's always something going on with a piggyback plant. This pretty little mama produces a 12-inch-tall mound of bright green, slightly fuzzy, broadly maplelike leaves, held upright on gently arching furred stems. Where the leaf attaches to its stem, mature foliage produces new plantlets that rise above the mother leaf on their own short stems. The resulting effect is quite charming as the mounded plant covers itself with new, smaller versions of its leaves and these dangle prettily over the edge of a pot or hanging basket.

Date I brought you home: _____

What I loved about you from the start: _____

Milestones in your growth: _____

HELP ME GROW

▶ Place your piggyback plant where it receives moderate to bright, filtered light. In nature, these plants live in moist, forest conditions and are not accustomed to full sun exposure.

▶ Cool to average home temperatures suit piggyback plant's needs and it doesn't mind temperatures as low as 50°F. In warmer locations, it will enjoy misting to provide extra humidity.

▶ Good-quality potting soil will satisfy your piggyback plant. A hanging basket shows off the new plantlets as they piggyback onto the mature leaves. Repot in spring to give your piggyback plant fresh potting mix.

FEED ME

▶ Water to maintain evenly, moderately moist soil conditions, allowing the top half inch of the mix to dry out in between drinks. Reduce watering somewhat in the winter, but don't let your piggyback plant dry out.

▶ Serve this busy mother-of-thousands a balanced houseplant fertilizer every 2–3 weeks during spring and into early fall. Reduce feedings to once per month during the winter months.

LOVE ME ♥

Another mother: "Mother-of-thousands" is a name given to other plants, including *Saxifraga stolonifera*, a.k.a. strawberry begonia, from the same family as piggyback plant, and *Kalanchoe daigremontiana*, a.k.a. devil's backbone. Like piggyback plant, these other mothers are so named for their prolific production of plantlets.

More, please: With all those plantlets, your mama piggyback may grow tired-looking after a couple of years. Fortunately, it's easy to grow a fresh, new version by rooting the many plantlets that arise from its leaves. Simply snip off a mature leaf with a well-developed plantlet on it, keeping about an inch of stem. Stick the stem into moist seed-starting medium so the base of the mother leaf where the plantlet arises is on the soil surface. Water very lightly until new growth signals that roots are forming. The old leaf will eventually dry up and can be carefully removed and the new plant potted up in a container of its own.

Pilea, aluminum plant
(Pilea cadierei)

If you're attracted to shiny things, the intricately decorated leaves of aluminum plant may earn it a place on your windowsill. Aluminum plant, also called watermelon pilea, is a handsome foliage plant with shallow-toothed, dark green leaves marked with raised silvery patches that give them a metallic appearance, while its leaf stems are touched with pink. This pretty plant grows 10–12 inches tall and gets along well in most household conditions. Aluminum plant blooms in summer and occasionally at other times, producing small clusters of insignificant, light-colored flowers at the tips of its stems.

Date I brought you home: _____

What I loved about you from the start: _____

Milestones in your growth: _____

HELP ME GROW

▶ Your aluminum plant will shine in moderate to bright, indirect or filtered light, and dislikes full, direct sun. Too little light will encourage stems to stretch and become leggy rather than leafy.

▶ Average room temperatures feel right to your aluminum plant and it will sulk if exposed to temperatures below 55°F. Its pretty leaves are thin and need humidity to look their best.

PLANTS IN GLASS HOUSES: A terrarium can be a happy place for your aluminum plant, providing it with draft-free warmth and the humidity it craves.

▶ A good-quality potting mix of soil and peat will satisfy this sprout. Aluminum plant's roots are not substantial and it will grow happily in a small and somewhat shallow pot. Repot in spring to freshen the soil, but consider taking cuttings of plants that grow gangly instead of repotting them. Aluminum plant's somewhat lax, bushy habit makes it an attractive choice for a hanging basket.

FEED ME

▶ Give frequent light drinks during the active growth period from spring to early fall, watering with room-temperature water to keep the potting soil lightly moist but never soggy. Water more moderately during the winter, allowing the top half inch of the soil to dry out between drinks.

▶ Serve your aluminum plant every 2–3 weeks from spring into fall with a balanced fertilizer diluted to half the recommended strength. Reduce feedings to monthly during the winter.

LOVE ME ♥

Aluminum recycling: As it ages, your aluminum plant will tend to shed its lower leaves and look more like a gangly teenager than an adorable bushy baby. Pinching back stem tips of aluminum plant in the spring will help encourage bushy growth, but you can also make cuttings from those stem tips and root them in seed-starting mix. In warm conditions and lightly moist medium, the cuttings will root within a month to create fresh new aluminum plants for you to love.

Poinsettia

(Euphorbia pulcherrima)

The bright-colored poinsettia that joins your family for the holidays may be more of a temporary guest than a long-lasting family member. Even so, showing it good hospitality will help it keep its good looks through the festive season and into the new year. Your poinsettia's display comes from its colorful bracts, modified leaf structures that are traditionally red but may be almost any color of the rainbow thanks to extensive breeding of this most popular holiday plant. The bracts fan out, flowerlike, around the actual flowers, which are small, yellow, and green. Healthy foliage is dark green with a visible central vein and may be variegated with splashes of creamy white.

Date I brought you home: _____

What I loved about you from the start: _____

Milestones in your growth: _____

HELP ME GROW

▶ Bright, indirect light is beneficial if your poinsettia's pretty bracts are still developing, but a plant in full display will be happy in almost any lighting except full sun, which can cause fading.

BRINGING BABY BACK: Plants being raised for a second year's display enjoy summer outdoors in bright, filtered light and need a specific light regimen to help them return to bloom.

▶ Cool, consistent conditions (60–70°F) are best for prolonging your plant's showy bracts.

WHEN THE HEAT IS ON: In a warm, heated space, keep your sprout away from vents. Moisten its air with a pebble tray and give its leaves an occasional misting.

▶ If you need to repot your poinsettia, it will be happy with any mix that drains well and retains even moisture. If your baby came in the usual plastic pot, dress it up with a decorative outer pot, making sure to raise it up on a layer of rocks to keep it from sitting in water.

FEED ME

▶ Water regularly to maintain evenly, lightly moist potting soil, allowing the top of the mix to dry out in between drinks, but never letting things become so dry that your poinsettia wilts.

DON'T BE FOILED: That shiny wrapper can be a glittering death trap without proper parental intervention. If you choose to keep the foil, poke holes in it to correspond to the drainage holes in the pot or cut away the bottom entirely. Be sure to put a saucer beneath the plant.

▶ A poinsettia that's just home for the holidays won't need much feeding, but young plants that are still developing their bracts will benefit from a fertilizer for flowering plants served every couple of weeks. If your relationship lasts past the holidays, resume fertilizing in spring, serving a balanced fertilizer every 3–4 weeks throughout the summer and switching to a flowering-plant formula in the fall.

LOVE ME

A *trick of the light*: Convincing a poinsettia to repeat its performance from last Christmas can be difficult. Keep your plant healthy with appropriate feeding and watering through the spring and summer, placing it in a shaded spot outdoors if possible until night temperatures begin dropping into the 50s. Eight to ten weeks of strict bedtimes and total darkness for 14 hours each night, paired with bright light during the day, are needed for your poinsettia to return to its former glory.

Polka dot plant
(Hypoestes phyllostachya)

Mounds of tidy, heart-shaped leaves spotted, speckled, or splashed with red, pink, or creamy white make the colorful polka dot plant too tempting for any would-be plant parent to resist. Take this adorable plant home and pair it with the showy veined foliage of nerve plant (*Fittonia*), which has similar care requirements. Keeping a polka dot plant happy takes a bit of effort to make sure it has the proper combination of high humidity and bright light it needs, but you'll know it's worth it when you admire its cheery freckled foliage.

Date I brought you home: _____

What I loved about you from the start: _____

Milestones in your growth: _____

HELP ME GROW

▶ Your little polka dot plant needs bright but indirect or filtered light to keep it happy. In too little light its pretty freckles will fade to green, while direct sun can make its leaves curl.

▶ Normal to warm room temperatures (65–80°F) and moderate to high humidity will keep your polka dot plant comfortable. Protect it from drafts and chilly air below 55°F as well as from drying air blowing from heating vents in the winter.

▶ A potting mix that provides good drainage is all your polka dot plant will ask. Although it enjoys humidity, it dislikes soggy conditions. Repot in spring or summer whenever roots begin to fill the pot; this sprout dislikes crowding in its container. A terrarium makes a nice home for polka dot plant, where it will enjoy the humid air.

FEED ME

▶ Water to maintain lightly moist soil conditions, allowing the top of the mix to dry out between drinks. Soggy soil will make your polka dot plant sulky. Both over- and underwatering can cause it to drop its pretty leaves.

▶ When your polka dot plant is actively growing and producing new leaves, feed it every 2–3 weeks with a balanced plant food diluted to half strength.

LOVE ME

Friends with fronds: Mix polka dot plant with ferns to add color to their greenery and keep your freckle-faced baby happy amid the shared humidity.

In a pinch: Polka dot plant reaches 10–12 inches tall indoors and benefits from occasional pinching to encourage branching, bushy growth. Your polka dot plant may bloom in early spring, but its small purplish flowers are unremarkable and should be pinched off. Even with corrective pinching, a polka dot plant will tend to grow leggy and bare-stemmed with age and may best be replaced with a fresh-faced youngster.

Ponytail palm
(Beaucarnea recurvata)

A big, dramatic plant, your ponytail palm is not truly a palm but a cousin of the yucca with a palmlike presence. Also called elephant's foot for its bulbous soil-level stem that supports a topknot of narrow, 3-foot-long foliage, beaucarnea stores moisture in its swollen trunk, making it easygoing in the watering department. Ponytail palm is a slow grower that proceeds with quiet dignity to achieve a height of 4–6 feet indoors. With modest care it will fill a large spot in your home and your heart for many years.

Date I brought you home: _____

What I loved about you from the start: _____

Milestones in your growth: _____

HELP ME GROW

▶ Your little ponytail palm will be at its best in bright lighting, although it can tolerate lower light for a few months in winter when its slow growth becomes even slower.

▶ Average household temperatures (60–75°F) meet ponytail palm's needs, and it is more tolerant of dry air than most houseplants.

▶ Cradle your ponytail palm's substantial stem in a fast-draining soil mix, such as one intended for cacti, with a significant sand content. Repot every 2–3 years to refresh its potting medium and increase container size when its thick stem grows within an inch or two of the edge of its pot. Replant at the same depth when repotting and avoid injuring the fleshy stem, which can let in rot organisms.

FEED ME

▶ Ponytail palm is a light drinker, even in the thirsty summertime. From spring through fall, water occasionally, when the top 2 inches of its potting soil are dry. Give it a drink even less often during the winter when lower light levels cause growth to slow to a crawl. Too much water in the winter is a greater danger to your ponytail palm's health than drying out.

▶ For a big sprout, your ponytail palm's appetite is modest. Feed it monthly from spring through the summer with a balanced houseplant fertilizer. Don't fertilize during fall and winter.

LOVE ME

Smooth moves: Even if your ponytail palm is only medium-sized when you bring it home, this sprout has growth potential. As it increases its height and diameter, the combined weight of plant, soil, and pot will grow, too. Plan ahead and get this baby some wheels (i.e., a set of castors), particularly if you want to move it outdoors for the summer and back again in the fall.

Good grooming: Your ponytail palm doesn't much mind dry air in the winter, but low humidity can make it prone to spider mite infestation. It's good parenting to inspect its long, strappy leaves every so often to make sure there are no pests hiding in that pretty ponytail. Give the foliage a refreshing spritz and wipe it clean of dust while you check for unwanted guests.

Pothos, golden pothos
(Epipremnum aureum)

Pretty vining pothos is pure gold for novice plant parents in need of an easy adoptee to give them confidence in their parenting skills. Pothos vines will ramble to 6 feet long bearing glossy 4- to 6-inch heart-shaped leaves that start out green but develop irregular golden yellow variegation. Some varieties of golden pothos offer increased yellow spotting and streaking on the foliage, and there are others with white-marked leaves, too. "Devil's ivy" is another nickname for pothos, perhaps because of its toxic sap that makes it a no-no (but not a deadly one) for curious nibblers.

Date I brought you home: _____

What I loved about you from the start: _____

Milestones in your growth: _____

HELP ME GROW

▶ Tolerance of a wide range of lighting situations is one reason for golden pothos's popularity. Your winning little sprout will shine in moderate to bright, indirect light, including under fluorescent lighting.

BRIGHTEN MY DAY: Lower light levels are not a deal breaker for golden pothos, but a plant that spends all its time in a dimly lit situation will likely grow slowly and lose its pretty golden variegation.

▶ Average household temperatures (60–80°F) and humidity suit golden pothos just fine.

▶ A potting mix with good drainage is all your pothos asks to find in its pot. Keep pot size close to the size of the root-ball to reduce the risk of overwatering. Repot annually in the spring. Your pothos will look pretty trailing from a hanging basket, draped from a planter on a high shelf, or climbing up a moss-covered support post.

FEED ME

▶ During spring and summer, let the top inch of your golden child's potting soil dry out in between waterings; water sparingly in winter to maintain barely moist soil. This handsome vine dislikes overwatering and will become sulky and inclined to drop its leaves if its roots are soggy.

▶ Feed every 2–3 weeks from spring into fall with a balanced fertilizer. Space feedings out to once a month during the winter.

LOVE ME

Shape my personality: A happy pothos is a vigorous vine that will benefit from a bit of parental pruning to keep it from sprawling too far. Prune off stem tips in spring (stick these in water and root them to make more sprouts to love!), cutting back to just beyond a healthy leaf. Gangly vines may be pruned back to 2–3 inches above the potting soil to encourage new sprouts to emerge.

Pin it up: With your help, your pothos can climb up rather than dangling down. Give it a trellis or a mossy or bark-clad post to clamber up, fastening it with twist ties, pins, or florist's tape in the direction you want it to grow. Golden pothos produces aerial roots but is not as clingy as some vines; it will depend on you to help it hold on as it grows upward.

Breathe easy: More than just a pretty vine, golden pothos is among the plants recognized by NASA for its ability to remove harmful chemicals such as volatile organic compounds (VOCs) and formaldehyde from indoor air.

Prayer plant
(Maranta leuconeura)

The lovely leaf markings of prayer plant may inspire you to meditate, but this pretty foliage plant is so called because of the way it folds its leaves in darkness and reopens them when exposed to light. The folded leaves remind some of hands folded in prayer. But this plant is inspiring even without that nifty trick, producing colorful 5-inch-long oval leaves with a satiny finish. Depending on its variety, your prayer plant's leaves may display reddish veins against a background of dark green brushed with lighter green or medium-green leaves with striking yellow venation. Prayer plant rarely blooms indoors, but you'll be so dazzled by its showy foliage that you won't miss its unremarkable flowers.

Date I brought you home: _____

What I loved about you from the start: _____

Milestones in your growth: _____

HELP ME GROW

▶ Place your prayer plant in moderate to bright but always indirect or filtered light. Full sun may scorch its leaves.

CUBICLE COMPANION: Your plant will be happy in bright fluorescent lighting, adding pizzazz to an office space.

▶ Average to warm room temperatures and moderate humidity keep your plant comfy. Give it a spot where temperatures range from 65–80°F and protect it from drafts and temperature fluctuations. A pebble tray to boost humidity is beneficial, especially during the winter.

▶ A rich but well-drained, peaty potting mix will snuggle your prayer plant's roots. Repot plants in spring, moving them into a slightly larger container and refreshing their potting soil. A shallow pot or dish garden is roomy enough for your prayer plant's modest root system.

FEED ME

▶ Give frequent drinks during the active growth period from spring to early fall, watering with room-temperature filtered or distilled water or with rainwater to keep the potting soil evenly but lightly moist and never soggy. Water more moderately during the winter, allowing the top half inch of the soil to dry out between drinks.

WATCH WATER QUALITY: Your prayer plant is sensitive about what's in its water. Serving it softened, fluoridated, or hard water can lead to browning.

▶ Feed every 2–3 weeks from spring through the summer with a balanced fertilizer mixed at half strength. Reduce feedings to once per month in the fall and winter.

LOVE ME

Rabbit tracks: *Maranta leuconeura* 'Kerchoveana' (or 'Kerchoviana') is a variety known as rabbit tracks for the rows of dark brown patches that line either side of each leaf's central vein.

Colorful kin: Your prayerful sprout will happily share care and space with closely related calathea, a similarly showy foliage plant that doesn't fold its leaves at night.

More, please: An overlarge prayer plant may be divided carefully in the spring to create more manageable-sized plants. Take care to get some roots with every piece and err on the side of making fewer large divisions rather than too many small pieces. Give extra TLC to the divided plants while they adjust to their new cribs. Mist foliage and put a plastic bag over each pot containing a new division, removing the cover after new roots have formed.

Sago palm

(*Cycas revoluta*)

Although it's not a true palm, sago palm can fill the role of one if you have a brightly lit open space to fill. This regal cycad's ancestors shared space with dinosaurs, and your not-so-petite sago palm will add a touch of the primeval to its place in your home. Sago palm produces a knobby, swollen, pineapple-like trunk that is crowned with an open rosette of arching, rigid, 3-foot fronds clad in dense rows of narrow, 3- to 6-inch-long leaflets. A slow grower, your sago palm has the potential to reach a height of 6 feet with similar spread, but will do so very gradually and may produce no more than one new leaf per year.

Date I brought you home: _____

What I loved about you from the start: _____

Milestones in your growth: _____

HELP ME GROW

▶ Your sago palm needs bright light to keep it happy and it will appreciate a few hours of direct sunlight daily during the winter months.

▶ Average room temperatures will keep your sago palm cozy, but it can tolerate cool conditions down to 55°F. It won't mind low indoor humidity the way many houseplants do, but take care to keep it out of the direct flow of warm air from a heating vent just the same.

▶ A potting mix that contains lots of sand and perlite to make it loose and fast-draining is what sago palm needs to keep its chunky base and the roots beneath it comfortable. Repot when the rusty brown base covers about two-thirds of the potting soil surface in your sago palm's container, handling carefully to avoid getting poked by the sharp, stiff leaflets.

FEED ME

▶ Your sago palm's swollen trunk base is a moisture storage structure that allows the plant to withstand occasional drought. Water moderately but thoroughly whenever your sago is actively growing. Let the top half inch to inch of potting soil dry out between waterings. During the winter, your cycad's already slow growth may slow even more. Letting the potting mix all but dry out during this time is preferable

to overwatering a sago palm that's having a brief winter rest.

▶ *Protect the crown:* When watering, avoid wetting your sago palm's rusty brown trunk and the crown where its leaves arise. Soggy conditions around its base can lead to rot.

▶ Feed monthly with a balanced fertilizer diluted to half strength from spring to early fall. Pause feeding during the winter.

LOVE ME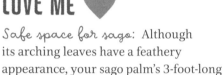

Safe space for sago: Although its arching leaves have a feathery appearance, your sago palm's 3-foot-long leaves are clothed in dozens of sharp, stiff, 3- to 6-inch leaflets that stick out in a V from the central leaf stalk. Sago palm's prickly nature means you need to take extra care in selecting its place in your home, making sure it is out of the path of traffic and where passersby are unlikely to brush against it.

Scarlet star

(Guzmania lingulata)

A fountain of glossy, strappy, deep green leaves surrounds the central cup of scarlet star, an attractive 10- to 12-inch-tall bromeliad. Mature plants bloom in late winter, producing a dramatic spike of brightly colored bracts that surround the small yellow flowers. Depending upon its variety, your little star's bracts may be bright red, pink, lavender, or yellow. Its flower display may shine for 6 or more weeks, giving you lots of time to dote on your pretty prodigy's achievement.

Date I brought you home:_____

What I loved about you from the start:_____

Milestones in your growth:_____

HELP ME GROW

▶ Your star can shine in less light than other bromeliads, even growing happily under bright fluorescent lighting. A spot in moderate to bright, indirect light will suit its needs. Although brighter is better to encourage it to bloom, scarlet star dislikes direct sun.

▶ Normal to warm household temperatures (65–80°F) year-round and high humidity are what your star needs to feel cozy. Prolonged time spent in temperatures below 55°F can make this pretty baby sulk. Provide a pebble tray and mist the leaves to keep its air moist.

▶ Give this sprout's roots good drainage and ample aeration with an orchid potting mix or one that combines equal parts peat moss or coir (coconut fiber) and leaf mold or potting soil. A shallow and somewhat small container is enough for scarlet star's modest root system. Repot in the spring to refresh its potting mix, increasing pot size only when needed.

FEED ME

▶ Water your scarlet star with filtered or distilled water or with rainwater. Bromeliads are sensitive to chemicals in softened water, while hard water will leave deposits on the foliage. Maintain water constantly in the central cup, turning the plant over once a month to empty old water, then sprinkling the leaves

and refilling the cup with a fresh drink. Moisten the medium around its roots to keep it lightly moist at all times.

▶ Serve your scarlet star a balanced liquid fertilizer diluted to half the recommended strength once a month, applying it to leaves, roots, and in its central cup.

LOVE ME

All grown up: When your scarlet star is 3–4 years old, it will be ready to produce its showy, long-lasting spike of flowers and colorful bracts. "Pups" (new plants) will form around its base as its blooms fade. Let these offsets grow to about one-third the size of their parent before separating them and planting.

A refreshing flush: Because water doesn't flow freely through your scarlet star's potting medium, residues from its monthly feedings can build up in the mix and in its pot. These salty fertilizer leftovers can harm delicate roots and diminish their ability to support your shining star. A thorough drenching of the pot and potting medium every summer will help clear away the remains of feedings past. Pour water into the pot until it runs out through the drainage holes, then let the pot drain for half an hour before repeating the process. Pour off all excess water after you're finished flushing.

Scented geraniums

(Pelargonium species and hybrids)

Close kin of the bright red geraniums that pour their showy flower clusters from hanging baskets, porch tubs, and window boxes throughout the summer, scented geraniums are grown for their wonderfully aromatic foliage. Although some types have delicately attractive blossoms, most scented geraniums are prized for their remarkably fragrant leaves. Species and hybrids may be found that feature citrus, herbal, floral, or spicy aromas that are released by rubbing or brushing their often slightly fuzzy leaves. Choose the scent you find most appealing and enjoy a green baby that provides companionship and aromatherapy in exchange for a modest amount of care.

Date I brought you home: _____

What I loved about you from the start: _____

Milestones in your growth: _____

HELP ME GROW

► Scented geraniums are sun lovers and yours will appreciate spending at least half of every day in direct sunlight while it is actively growing. In winter, it will tolerate lower light while it is resting.

SUMMER IN THE SUN: If your plant gets to spend time outside during the summer, it will enjoy bright shade, morning sunshine, or filtered sunlight. In fall, move it gradually into lower lighting to prepare it to return indoors.

► Cool to normal household temperatures and average humidity are fine for scented geraniums.

► Well-drained, peaty potting soil keeps scented geraniums happy. Repot plants annually in the spring, gently shaking old soil from the roots and lightly pruning roots before replanting in fresh mix. Growing your baby in a small container will help keep the plant compact.

FEED ME

► Let the top half inch of your scented geranium's soil dry out between drinks from spring into early fall. Cut back on watering during the winter months, providing just enough to keep the soil from drying out completely.

► Serve your sweet-scented sprout a balanced houseplant fertilizer every 2 weeks from spring into early fall. Pause feeding during the winter months while baby takes a rest from active growth.

LOVE ME

Put me down for a nap: Lower light levels and cooler temperatures will prompt your scented geranium to pause for a bit in the winter months. A cool "nap" at temperatures from 50–60°F will help it rest. Give it just enough water to keep your sprout from shriveling and its potting mix from drying out entirely. Do not fertilize while baby is resting.

What's that smell? You can wear out your sniffer during a visit to a greenhouse that features scented geraniums. The range of available fragrances offers something for almost every olfactory preference and many hybrids have attractive deeply lobed leaves or felted gray-green foliage. Once you get to know these aromatic plants, you may be tempted to adopt several. Among the most popular fragrances are rose, lemon, cinnamon, nutmeg, and patchouli.

More, please: Over a few years' time, your scented geranium may become leggy, in spite of your loving care. Save the situation by taking 3-inch stem tip cuttings in the spring from fresh new growth and rooting them in moistened seed-starting mix to create new compact versions of your favorite aromatic plant.

Shamrock plant, false shamrock, oxalis
(Oxalis regnellii, Oxalis triangularis)

A cheery shamrock plant might come into your home around St. Patrick's Day when stores are filled with these faux clovers. But no luck is needed to enjoy the year-round company of oxalis's triangular leaflets and delicate white or pink flowers. Oxalis varieties may have green leaves trimmed in silver or with purple undersides or rich purple foliage with lighter mauve markings. Tiny tubers known as pips are beneath the pretty profusion of a pot of oxalis. With modest care, shamrock will make you feel like a lucky plant parent as you enjoy its steady display of foliage and flowers.

Date I brought you home: _____

What I loved about you from the start: _____

Milestones in your growth: _____

HELP ME GROW

▶ Moderate to bright, filtered or indirect light will satisfy your shamrock's needs.

KEEP ME COLORFUL: Oxalis with purple or variegated foliage will display their best leafy features when placed in a well-lit location.

▶ Normal room temperatures (60–75°F) and average household humidity keep shamrock plant comfortable.

▶ Well-drained potting soil is all this little shamrock needs. Repot when things get crowded in the container, replanting the pinecone-like tubers 2 inches deep in fresh potting mix.

FEED ME

▶ Water to maintain lightly moist soil, allowing just the top of the potting mix to dry out between sprinklings.

DRY AND DROWSY: If your oxalis's container dries out, it may trigger a period of dormancy, during which the top growth all dies back. Don't give up on your shamrock plant if this happens. Cut off the faded foliage and repot the pips. Water lightly until new growth appears, usually within 4–6 weeks.

▶ Feed every 2–4 weeks with a balanced houseplant fertilizer. Don't feed shamrock plants during dormancy.

LOVE ME ❤

A *nifty leaf trick*: Watch your oxalis as night falls—it will fold its pretty leaves and close its flowers in darkness and open them again in the light of day.

Unlucky for Rover and Fluffy: Shamrock plant is toxic to pets. Discourage curious nibblers and place your shamrock plant where it's unlikely to tempt fur siblings to sample it.

More, please: Oxalis is so easy to increase by simply dividing the clump of bulbs into smaller clusters and replanting the divisions in fresh soil in their own pots. You can create shamrock plants to share at any time, during dormancy or active growth. After dividing or repotting, trim off faded or broken leaves. Water sparingly and pause feeding until fresh growth resumes.

Snake plant

(Sansevieria trifasciata)

Though it's a rather forbidding-looking plant with sharply pointed sword-shaped leaves, you still may be tempted to hug your snake plant when you discover how easy it is to care for. This 1- to 2-foot-tall succulent, also called mother-in-law's tongue (because it's sharp, get it?), produces a group of thick, glossy, subtly striped dark green leaves that may be edged with yellow or creamy white. Your snake plant can survive in spite of neglect, but it will reward the care you give it with long-lasting, dramatic good looks.

Date I brought you home: _____

What I loved about you from the start: _____

Milestones in your growth: _____

HELP ME GROW

▶ Your snake plant will bask in bright, indirect or filtered light from spring into fall. During the winter, its light needs are more modest. Too much time in low lighting can cause your snake plant's variegated leaves to fade to all green.

▶ Average room temperatures (65–80°F) are cozy for your plant any time of year.

DON'T CHILL ME: While it won't mind a rest period at the cool end of its range in the winter, temperatures below 55–60°F will make a snake plant sulky.

▶ A sandy potting mix meant for cacti will keep your plant's roots comfortable. Choose a heavy container to help balance the weight of its sturdy leaves. But don't go overlarge. Your snake plant likes its root zone snug and too much space will make it prone to overwatering. Add stones to the bottom of the pot to provide additional weight. Repot in spring only when the container is very crowded.

FEED ME

▶ During active growth in the spring and summer, water moderately to thoroughly moisten its potting mix, then let the top inch of soil dry out before the next drink. During the winter, water infrequently, allowing the soil to dry out almost completely between drinks.

I LIKE IT DRY: Leaves that turn entirely yellow are a sign of overwatering, while wrinkled leaves are a sign that your plant is too dry. When watering, avoid pouring water into the middle of your plant's cluster of leaves, and don't let water linger at the base of its foliage.

▶ Keep your snake plant on a modest diet, serving it a balanced fertilizer mixed at half strength once a month from spring into fall. Pause feeding during the winter when baby is resting.

LOVE ME

Take a breath: Your sansevieria will earn its keep by cleaning the air of volatile organic compounds (VOCs) and other common indoor air pollutants.

Grow a spear: A close relative of snake plant, African spear (*Sansevieria cylindrica*) produces a cluster of cylindrical, sharply pointed leaves with gray-green marbled coloring. Care is the same as for snake plant.

More, please: Divide in early spring when your snake plant has produced new growth that is at least 6 inches tall around its base. Use a sturdy knife to cut through its thick rhizome to separate a cluster of leaves with roots attached. Sansevierias also may be propagated by leaf cuttings, but these take much longer to develop roots and grow to full-sized plants.

Spider plant

(Chlorophytum comosum)

A hanging basket brimming with the arching, fountain-like foliage of a healthy spider plant and ringed by shoots bearing starry white flowers and dangling spider "babies" is a beautiful sight and one that's easy to achieve for even the least experienced plant parents. If you're itching to start a big plant family, a spider plant makes a perfect adoptee, as these easy-care plants can begin producing plantlets of their own when they are under a year old. Display your burgeoning family of spider plant and plantlets from a hanging basket or atop a pedestal or shelf that allows its babies to swing prettily on their stems.

Date I brought you home: _____

What I loved about you from the start: _____

Milestones in your growth: _____

HELP ME GROW

▶ Bright lighting is best for maintaining your spider plant's leaf color, whether it is white- or yellow-striped or solid green. A few hours of morning sun will be welcomed in the winter months, but direct summer sun is too strong and can scorch the foliage.

▶ Your spider plant can tolerate a broad range of temperatures from 50–75°F but will be happiest in moderate conditions. Spending time below 55°F will slow its growth and make it prone to root rot, while very warm temperatures increase its need for humidity and can cause dry brown tips on its leaves.

▶ Spider plants are happy in any good potting soil. Repot annually in the spring or when your sprout's fleshy roots have pushed their potting mix up to the rim of the pot. Move into a larger container to give your plant room to stretch its roots.

FEED ME

▶ Evenly moist soil from spring through summer will make your spider plant happy. Give your baby rainwater or distilled or filtered water; spider plants may develop brown leaf tips in response to fluoride or chlorine in treated tap water. In fall and winter, reduce watering to allow the top inch of its potting soil to dry out between waterings.

▶ Feed your spider plant every 2–3 weeks from spring through summer with a balanced fertilizer diluted to half strength. Pause feedings in winter.

LOVE ME

Shower me: Give your plant a shower of tepid water now and then to rinse and refresh its foliage and flush out any pests.

Turn up the dark: Spider plants bloom in response to shortening day length and may resist putting forth flower stems and plantlets if they spend their evenings in artificial lighting. To prompt your plant to start making babies, let it spend time outdoors in the fall as daylight decreases or give it a few weeks in a room where there's no lighting after dark in the fall and winter.

More, please: Look for a plantlet with 2- to 3-inch-long leaves and the beginnings of roots and snip it from the stem attaching it to the parent plant. Remove any lower leaves around the roots and suspend it with its developing roots in water. When its roots grow to an inch long, plant it in soil in a pot of its own. You can also leave a plantlet attached, pinning it (with a bent paper clip or similar) to the surface of a small pot of potting soil placed next to the parent plant. Within 6 weeks the plantlet should be well rooted and may be separated from its parent.

Spotted laurel
(Aucuba japonica)

A treelike plant with glossy green leaves, the spotted laurel is a handsome baby that will brighten your days with its golden-freckled foliage. In warm temperate areas, spotted laurel grows into a 6- to 15-foot shrub in shady locations, but its indoor version is unlikely to exceed 3 feet tall. Selections with more or less gold variegation on its leaves are available to bring a splash of color to a spot where less hardy plants might struggle. Your spotted laurel may produce unremarkable purple flowers in the summer.

Date I brought you home: _____

What I loved about you from the start: _____

Milestones in your growth: _____

HELP ME GROW

► Give your spotted laurel a place where it can enjoy bright, filtered sunlight year-round.

► Spotted laurel doesn't mind chilly temperatures and is a good choice for a drafty entryway or a bright, cool porch; it will be most comfortable where temperatures range from 50–65°F. In warm indoor temperatures (70°F and up), it will suffer and sulk and require high humidity to keep it comfortable.

► Tuck your spotted laurel's roots into a good soil-based potting medium. Keep its pot on the snug side relative to its root mass and increase its pot size only when its roots become crowded in the container. Repot in spring when needed. Once your sprout reaches a 10- to 12-inch pot, refresh the top layer of the potting mix each spring.

PROVIDE BALANCE: As your spotted laurel grows tall and bushy in comparison to its cozy container, keep it in a heavy pot or anchor it somehow to prevent it from toppling over and breaking its branches.

FEED ME

► Consistent, even soil moisture is necessary to keep little spotted laurel happy but avoid letting it sit in a soggy pot.

► Serve up monthly portions of balanced fertilizer to your spotted laurel to keep its freckled leaves looking their best.

LOVE ME

All that glitters: Good grooming will help your spotted laurel's gold-dusted leaves sparkle and gives you the chance to monitor its health and spot any problems before they get out of hand. Gently wipe baby's glossy leaves with a damp cloth to clean off dust and grime, checking leaf undersides and stems for pests such as spider mites and scale.

Spring pruning: If your spotted laurel likes its place in your home so much that it threatens to outgrow its space, cut its branches back in early spring to curb its enthusiasm. Prune back to just above a pair of leaves to promote branching and bushy growth.

Staghorn fern
(Platycerium bifurcatum)

An epiphytic fern with rainforest origins, staghorn fern bears broad fronds that may stretch to 3 feet long with antlerlike lobed edges. These "antler" fronds arise from a flat, rounded shield frond that grows over the fern's roots and whatever they're attached to. The overall effect of this dramatic fern is sort of a vegetarian version of a rack of antlers mounted on the wall. A staghorn fern presents challenges for even an experienced plant parent, but providing it with the specialized care it requires can create a unique bond with this unusual plant.

Date I brought you home: _____

What I loved about you from the start: _____

Milestones in your growth: _____

HELP ME GROW

▶ Bright, filtered light such as the sunlight coming through leafy branches is staghorn fern's favorite. Direct sun, however, is too much and can scorch.

▶ Your staghorn fern needs cool to average room temperatures (55–70°F) and abundant humidity. Daily misting is a necessity to keep your staghorn fern comfortable in most indoor locations.

▶ Staghorn fern grows best when attached to a rough bark support or "planted" in a wooden basket filled with peat and sphagnum moss. If grown in a pot, it will do best in an orchid potting mix, but this is only satisfactory for young, small staghorns. Mount or hang your staghorn fern where it will enjoy the light and humidity it needs as well as good ventilation, but keep it accessible for daily misting and thorough watering.

FEED ME

▶ It's important to thoroughly moisten the root system and surrounding medium, but water must also be allowed to drain away, making the process rather messy for most indoor locations. Try immersing the plant's support and attached roots in a large container of tepid water for 15–20 minutes at a time during the spring and summer when the fern is actively growing, then let it drip-dry before returning it to its usual location. A fern kept in a warm, dry room may need to be watered this way once per week, while cool, humid conditions may allow watering every 2–3 weeks. Follow your fern's lead: watch for drooping fronds and lightweight (dry) growing medium.

WHEN I'M RESTING: Water more sparingly in the winter when your staghorn is not actively growing, following the same dunking process but only for a minute or two at a time.

▶ Feed a mature staghorn fern once a month during the spring and summer by immersing its roots and supporting bark in a dilute liquid fertilizer for about 5 minutes. Do not feed resting plants.

LOVE ME

Don't mind the drips: Because the watering and fertilizing process involves applying liquid to a permeable container, the result can be a bit messy on surfaces below. Plan accordingly and accept that parenting a staghorn fern involves trade-offs to enjoy the beauty.

Protect the shield: The round shield frond at the base of your staghorn fern is always growing and being replaced by a new frond, which appears as a silvery green spot that expands to cover the brown papery old ones. Don't be alarmed when the shield frond begins to turn brown and papery, and don't try to remove it.

Strawberry begonia
(Saxifraga stolonifera)

If your vision of plant parenthood includes raising a large family, a dainty but prolific strawberry begonia may make a perfect addition to your happy home. One of several plants known by the common name "mother-of-thousands," strawberry begonia earns that title by producing abundant plantlets, miniature versions of itself borne on slender reddish runners. A low-growing plant, strawberry begonia bears its rounded, scalloped leaves in a rosette on 4-inch stalks. Its leaves are rich green with silvery contrasting veins and purple-red undersides; both the leaves and their reddish stems are covered in soft hairs. Flower spikes carrying clusters of small, starry white flowers appear in spring and summer.

Date I brought you home: _____

What I loved about you from the start: _____

Milestones in your growth: _____

HELP ME GROW

▶ Place your strawberry begonia where it will get plenty of bright light, including, if possible, a few hours of direct morning sun. Good lighting is especially important for varieties with white-variegated leaves.

BLOCK THE BURN: Don't go overboard with sunshine for your sprout. Overexposure to full, hot sun can cause scorching on its pretty leaves.

▶ Play it cool for your strawberry begonia's comfort, keeping it in a room where temperatures range from 50–70°F. Able to grow outdoors in warm temperate areas, it is happiest in cool indoor conditions. At the warm end of its preferred temperature range, it benefits from the extra humidity of a pebble tray under its pot.

▶ Plant your strawberry begonia in a sandy or perlite-rich potting mix to ensure its roots are never soggy. Repot annually in the spring. A hanging basket allows this speedy grower's abundant plantlets to dangle prettily from their long runners.

FEED ME

▶ From spring through summer, water to maintain lightly moist soil, allowing the top inch of the potting mix to dry out between watering. Water less frequently in winter when your strawberry begonia will enjoy a few weeks' rest in a cool location.

WATER FROM THE BOTTOM: Watering from below by setting the container in water for 30 minutes, then letting the excess drain away, helps protect your sprout from rot that can result from soggy conditions at the base of leaves and stems.

▶ Monthly feedings with a balanced houseplant fertilizer in spring and summer will satisfy your baby. Feed every 6–8 weeks during fall and winter.

LOVE ME

Help me bloom: A winter rest in 50–60°F temperatures with bright light, reduced watering, and no feeding for about a month will help put your strawberry begonia in the mood to bloom when spring arrives.

Youth culture: After a few years, your strawberry begonia's stems will develop woody bases that are inclined to rot. At this point, encourage one or more of its plantlets to root and grow a fresh, young replacement for your original plant.

More, please: More pretty strawberry begonias are yours for the taking. Use a bent paper clip to pin a plantlet to the surface of a small container of potting mix placed next to the mother plant. Rooting should take place within 3 weeks, at which time you can clip the runner and care for the new little plant as you have for its parent.

Succulents

Succulents include a diverse collection of sprouts with fleshy leaves, stems, and roots that allow them to store water to keep them alive through extended dry periods. Close kin of cacti, succulents generally are less prickly, although many feature spines to keep thirsty animals at bay in their native habitats. While it's hard to generalize about a group that encompasses the stiffly upright foliage of sansevieria (page 181) and the low-growing fleshy structures of living stones (page 194), many succulents have thick, often waxy foliage and rosette forms that help them collect moisture.

Date I brought you home: _____

What I loved about you from the start: _____

Milestones in your growth: _____

You are a: _____

HELP ME GROW

▶ Bright light, including daily full sun exposure, is in order for nearly all species of succulents. A few types prefer indirect light, and many will require a shady location if you move them outdoors for the summer.

MAKING SMART MOVES: Summer outside can satisfy your succulent's need for bright lighting, but going too quickly from indoors to out can give your sprout too much of a good thing. Make moves gradually, going from indoors to a shady outdoor spot and then perhaps to partial sun over a period of a few weeks. Reverse this process when it's time to move back indoors, making sure to start before the weather turns cold.

▶ Average to warm household temperatures work well for succulents most of the year but can be too cozy in winter when a cool rest period is in order for your succulent sprout. Although these plants are adapted to life in arid conditions, winter in a warm, dry home can stress a succulent. Occasionally misting your succulent sprout can help it keep its composure.

▶ Excellent drainage is the main requirement of any potting mixture for succulents. Mixtures designed for cacti are widely available or you can blend your own using potting soil well amended with coarse sand and/or perlite. Repot plants in spring, refreshing their potting soil and moving into a larger pot as needed.

HANDLE WITH CARE: Fleshy succulents can be quite brittle, making it easy to damage them when repotting. Be gentle when working with your sweet succulent. If necessary, wrap a towel or soft cloth around it to cushion it during potting operations.

FEED ME

▶ Water needs vary among succulents, but it's worth noting that your sprout will be far more forgiving of underwatering than overwatering. During the time when your succulent baby is actively growing, frequent light drinks will keep it happier than deep soaking ones, and soggy soil is never desirable. Winter watering should be even more sporadic and only enough to keep the soil from drying out entirely. But watch for signs that low humidity is taking a toll and consider a light mist on your sprout's foliage instead of watering its potting soil.

▶ **DON'T WET THE ROSETTE:** Succulents often grow in a rosette shape that creates channels to capture and collect scarce moisture in their natural environments. In your home, these water-catching capabilities can go wrong if water is applied too frequently to the top of the plant. Water from below or carefully on the potting soil rather than pouring water into your sprout's rosette of leaves.

▶ Once a month, serve your succulent a modest diet of cacti-focused fertilizer or balanced houseplant fertilizer mixed at half strength when it is actively growing in spring and summer. Pause feeding during fall and winter.

LOVE ME

AEONIUMS (*AEONIUM* SPECIES AND HYBRIDS)

Pinwheels and mini trees: There's something almost Seussian about the spoonlike, often unusually colored foliage of aeoniums, especially when it's borne in rosetted tufts on woody stems. Your little aeonium may have a treelike form but will likely remain under 2 feet tall with a similar spread. Pinwheel (*Aeonium haworthii*) has branching, woody stems topped by rosettes of fleshy gray-green leaves. Varieties of pinwheel have red-, pink-, or yellow-edged foliage. Other species and hybrids produce dense rosettes of deep purple to nearly black foliage that form loose, dramatic towers up to 2 feet tall.

Bloom and die: Aeoniums bloom at maturity, around 4–5 years old, producing sprays of starry, creamy yellow or pink flowers from the center of their rosettes. After flowering, individual rosettes will die, but plants consisting of multiple rosettes will continue growing as long as some do not produce flowers.

You can propagate an aeonium that's getting floppy and top-heavy by clipping off a young, healthy rosette with an inch of stem and rooting it in a seed-starting medium.

DONKEY'S TAIL, BURRO'S TAIL (*SEDUM MORGANIANUM*)

Giddyup: The trailing stems of this popular sedum are covered with rows of overlapping greenish-gray, jelly-bean-sized leaves, creating an effect deemed by imaginative plant lovers like that of a burro's ropy tail. However you feel about its equine namesakes, a hanging container dripping with this handsome plant looks glorious in a sunny window. Sedums generally appreciate full sun, but your donkey's tail will need a bit of shade to prevent sunburn on its juicy leaves if it goes outside in the summer. Burro's tail that gets too little light will produce straggly stems with sparse leaves.

No horsing around: Place your burro's tail in a spot where it can be admired but not jostled. The fleshy leaves that drape this succulent's lax stems break off easily if the plant gets bumped. This can make moving or repotting large plants tricky, although a happy donkey's tail will develop new stems to fill in where others have broken off. Take tip cuttings from healthy "tails" to root and create new plants when your original one outgrows your ability to handle it easily.

Cut off a 3-inch tip and remove the leaves from the lower 2 inches of stem; stick it into moist seed-starting mix to root.

LIVING STONES, SPLIT ROCKS (*LITHOPS* SPECIES)

Nubby and nice: Low- and slow-growing, each lithops plant consists of a pair of thick, flat-topped leaves that rise an inch or two above the soil surface from a short underground stem. The mottled coloring that makes living stones look like the rocks they naturally grow among comes from translucent "windows" on their surface that help them collect the light they need. Admire your little living stones in a bright site where they will enjoy 3 or 4 hours of direct sunlight during the summer months. Let this unusual plant's curious life cycle guide your care and it will be a beloved member of your family for many years.

When to water: Like most succulents, your living stones plant has minimal water needs. Follow its lead to avoid overwatering that will cause it to rot. A lithops needs a cool (50–70°F) rest period in winter, when it also needs bright but indirect light. While it's resting, keep it very dry and water lightly only if it gets very wrinkled. New leaves will emerge from the cleft in your lithops's surface in late winter or early spring, using the moisture from the old leaves to fuel their growth. No watering is necessary until the old leaves have shriveled away—by late spring, when you can lightly moisten the potting mix. Let your living stone's soil remain quite dry through the summer. In late summer to fall, a mature lithops will produce a daisylike flower from the cleft between its leaves. Water to just moisten its soil, letting the top two-thirds of the mix dry out in between drinks from the time when a bud appears until the flower fades. From fall through the winter, let your lithops enjoy its well-earned rest and very minimal watering.

STRING OF PEARLS (*SENECIO ROWELYANUS*)

A jewel for your windowsill: Slender stems "strung" with almost perfectly round pea- to marble-sized leaves that look like green pearls make this easy-care succulent a popular conversation piece for display in a hanging basket or a low, broad pot. Your pretty string of pearls's stems may stretch to 24 inches, bubbling over the rim of its container with leafy enthusiasm. Bright light, warm temperatures, and very modest watering will keep it happy; a cool rest period during the winter may prompt the production of insignificant white flowers in spring.

Pass these peas: Also called bead plant, this senecio is mildly toxic and can cause irritation and tummy upset in pets and curious humans that sample its tempting round leaves. Display string of pearls out of the reach of fur siblings and others who might mistake its pearls for peas or candy.

More, please: String of pearls's stems can produce roots at the points where leaves attach, making it simple to grow more of this amicable sprout. You can snip off any stems that are sparsely adorned with pearls to tidy your baby, but take a 3-inch cutting from the tip of a young, healthy strand for propagation purposes. Lay the cutting on top of a small pot of moist seed-starting mix and press the leaves into the mix until they are partially covered.

TIGER'S JAWS (*FAUCARIA TIGRINA*)

Fierce-looking but friendly: You need not fear the bite of this tiny, spiny tiger. Topping out at about 6 inches tall, tiger's jaws forms a low-growing rosette of pointed, sometimes speckled fleshy leaves that have curved, toothlike spines along their edges. The effect may be fierce, but the spines are soft and pose little risk. Keep your pretty tiger's jaws in a warm, sunny spot throughout the summer; it will enjoy spending time outdoors while it is actively growing. A cool, bright place to rest in the winter will make it purr, but avoid chilly temperatures below 60°F. Mature tiger's jaws may bloom in the fall if they've soaked up enough sunlight during the summer.

Care and feeding: Only feed your tiger's jaws lightly during spring and summer when it is actively growing, serving it a cactus food or dilute balanced fertilizer once a month. Keep its shallow roots in a modest container to avoid the risk of overwatering posed by too much soil relative to roots. Repot in early spring when the rosettes of triangular leaves cover the surface of their container. You can divide crowded tiger's jaws by separating rosettes from the original plant. Let cut surfaces dry for a day before giving the baby tiger's jaws pots of their own to prowl.

Swedish ivy

(Plectranthus australis)

A fuzzy-leaved member of the mint family, Swedish ivy is a popular plant for hanging baskets, which display its trailing, leafy stems to good effect. A container filled with this good-natured and easy-to-grow plant will brighten any room and serve as a visual counterpoint to vertical or large-leaved plant companions. Swedish ivy produces medium-green, rounded, gently pointed leaves with scalloped edges. A variegated form has attractive white-rimmed leaves. Spikes of small white to pink flowers may rise above the leaves in early summer; you can enjoy them or pinch them off if you don't like their looks.

Date I brought you home: _____

What I loved about you from the start: _____

Milestones in your growth: _____

HELP ME GROW

▶ Moderate to bright lighting suits Swedish ivy's needs. In very bright conditions its foliage may look a little washed out.

SUMMER IN THE SHADE: In the summer, Swedish ivy makes a happy container plant outdoors, where it will thrive in bright light but shaded from direct sun. Plants that have a "vacation" are more likely to bloom.

▶ Cool to average room temperatures (60–75°F) will keep your Swedish ivy comfortable. In warmer conditions, it will benefit from a bit of increased humidity, but this sprout is generally accepting of normal household conditions.

▶ Good-quality potting soil that permits good drainage is all your Swedish ivy needs to be comfortable in its container. Repot in spring or summer; your Swedish sprout is a vigorous grower that will fill its pot readily. Give it a hanging basket or a tall pot that lets its leafy stems dangle attractively over the edges.

FEED ME

▶ Water moderately to maintain evenly moist soil throughout the spring and summer when your Swedish ivy child is in active growth mode. Mint family members like moist conditions, but avoid letting the soil get soggy.

HANGING OUT, TOO DRY: Keep a close eye on watering in the summer when a vigorous Swedish ivy growing in a sunny spot may need a drink almost daily. Sunshine and air moving around a hanging basket can dry it out quickly and your sprout can become thirsty before you know it.

▶ Serve your pretty ivy a meal of balanced houseplant fertilizer every 2–3 weeks from spring through summer. Slow feeding to once a month during the fall and winter.

LOVE ME

Pinch me: Swedish ivy's typically abundant growth lends itself to parental shaping to help it look its best. Pinching back stem tips after your ivy blooms will encourage it to produce more branching, leafy growth, leading to a full, bushy plant. Pinch off faded flower spikes to keep baby tidy and prune damaged or unhealthy stems at any time.

More, please: After a few years, your Swedish ivy may become sprawling and less leafy, no matter how diligently you pinch and prune it. Stem tip cuttings of this plant will root easily in moist seed-starting mix or in water to start your sprout afresh. You can also divide your Swedish ivy when repotting in the spring, pruning it back when you do to stimulate fresh, bushy growth.

Ti plant

(Cordyline terminalis)

A young ti plant looks like a fountain of deep purple-red leaves rising from the soil.
Over time, your little ti will develop a short stem that will grow longer and more
trunk-like as the plant loses some of its lower leaves. This results in a slender plant
up to 5 feet tall with a topknot of lance-shaped leaves that may be 4 inches wide
and 18 inches long. Also called good luck tree or plant and Hawaiian or Polynesian
ti plant, this tropical is believed to bring good luck when placed near an entrance.
Varieties feature leaves variegated with bronze, pink, cream, and light green.

Date I brought you home: _____

What I loved about you from the start: _____

Milestones in your growth: _____

HELP ME GROW

▶ Your lucky ti plant needs bright light to maintain the color and variegation of its leaves. Place it where it will get up to 4 hours of direct sun each day.

▶ Keep your ti cozy in normal to warm household temperatures (60–85°F) and mist its narrow, pointed leaves daily to increase the humidity around it, especially at warmer room temperatures.

▶ Potting mix that drains well will meet your ti plant's needs. Repot every year or two in the spring, increasing the size of the container until it reaches an 8- to 10-inch diameter. A pot that's a little snug will make your ti plant happy, but choose a container with heft (or add a layer of rocks in the bottom) to ensure that your lucky ti doesn't tip over when it grows tall with all its leaves at the top.

FEED ME

▶ Keep your ti plant's potting soil evenly moist (but not soggy) during spring and summer when it is actively growing. If its leaf tips and edges turn brown, your ti may be feeling sad about fluoride in its water or it may be that the air is too dry. Switch to filtered water or rainwater for your sprout and keep up with misting or other humidifying methods. During the winter, reduce watering, letting the top inch of soil dry out between drinks.

▶ Feed every 2–3 weeks with a balanced houseplant fertilizer through the spring and summer. Fertilize monthly during fall and winter.

LOVE ME

Lucky me: Groom your little ti by gently wiping its handsome leaves with a damp cloth occasionally to keep them clean. This gives you the chance to check for spider mites or any other signs your good luck might be waning.

More, please: One of the reasons behind ti plant's reputation for luck is its ability to grow from what appears to be an unremarkable piece of stem. This simple start of a good luck plant used to be a common item available at flower shows. If your ti plant grows too tall and leggy for your liking, you can cut it off, leaving about 2 inches of the stem. A new plant will likely sprout from that stump. Cut 2- to 3-inch sections of the stem, making sure each piece has a bud (a swelling beneath the bark) and noting which end is the bottom or lower one. "Plant" these stem cuttings in moist potting medium and keep them warm and moist until sprouting occurs.

Tillandsias, air plants
(Tillandsia species and hybrids)

Is your heir plant an air plant? Tillandsias, also called air plants, are epiphytic bromeliads that take their moisture and nutrients through scales on their green-gray leaves. Their roots, if they have any, are typically sparse and wiry and used mainly as anchors to hold the plant's rosette of narrow, arching leaves in place on a branch or similar perch. An air plant may seem like the ultimate easy-care choice for uncertain plant parents, but these pot-free plantlings require regular attention to keep them alive and well.

Date I brought you home: _____

What I loved about you from the start: _____

Milestones in your growth: _____

HELP ME GROW

▶ Give your little air plant a spot where it enjoys bright, filtered light. In winter, it will even welcome a few hours of direct sun, but summer sun is too strong.

▶ Normal to warm household temperatures (65–80°F) and high humidity keep air plants comfortable. While chilly temperatures below 55–60°F may injure your air plant, a winter rest at around 65°F is beneficial for blooming.

▶ No pot or soil is required for your air plant's almost nonexistent roots. You can tuck it into a dab of sphagnum moss and use florist's wire (or a bent paper clip) to pin it to a piece of bark or driftwood or almost any object you like. A small, moss-lined basket can help with maintaining humidity.

FEED ME

▶ Mist your air plant a few times per week, wetting it completely. Use tepid, filtered or distilled water or rainwater. You may also give your plant a weekly soak for up to an hour, then let it drain before returning it to its perch. Make sure any watering dries within 4 hours; extended moisture can lead to rotting.

▶ Spritz-feed this airy sprout every 2 or 3 weeks with a dilute flowering-plant fertilizer. Feed from spring through summer, then pause fertilizing during the winter while your baby is resting.

LOVE ME ♥

Pink quill: Larger than many air plants, pink quill (*Tillandsia cyanea*) may be grown in a pot filled with orchid potting medium. Pink quill's leaves may grow 12–18 inches long, and it gets its name from the flattened, oval flower head of stiff pink bracts that rise 4–6 inches from the center of the plant's leafy rosette. Purple-blue flowers bloom from between the bracts.

The end of an air (plant): Air plants may bloom when they reach maturity, at around 3–5 years, producing a dense spike of bracts from the center of the rosette. The actual flowers peek out from between the bracts. Once an air plant blooms, its rosette dies, but offsets will form around the base and can be separated when they are one-third the size of the air parent plant.

Open a branch office: A small collection of air plants mounted on a branch or moss-stuffed wire form makes an appealing display of living art. With a bit of moss to enhance humidity or just on its own, an air plant may be tucked into all sorts of supporting containers, from shells and teacups to pieces of coral or cork. Just remember that any holder for your air plant should be moisture-resistant and placed where drips and mist are not a concern.

Umbrella tree, schefflera

(Schefflera species)

The glossy oval leaflets of scheffleras fan out from a central point like the spokes of an umbrella, earning this bushy, treelike plant its common name, umbrella tree. If you have a space in your home and your heart for a big, bold, tropical plant, a statuesque umbrella tree (*Schefflera actinophylla*) may be the perfect foliar family member for you. Would-be plant parents looking for a somewhat smaller sprout to love can enjoy the same handsomely leafy effects of the dwarf schefflera (*Schefflera arboricola*), a bushier umbrella tree with 4-inch leaflets and mature height of up to 5 feet.

Date I brought you home: _____

What I loved about you from the start: _____

Milestones in your growth: _____

HELP ME GROW

▶ Place your umbrella tree in a spot with bright, indirect or filtered light. Direct sun is too much for schefflera's broad foliage. Types with variegated leaves will fade to green in too little light.

TAKE YOUR SPROUT TO WORK: An umbrella tree can be happy under fluorescent lighting, making it a good choice as an office companion.

▶ Protect your schefflera from chilly drafts and temperatures below 55°F. Average to warm room temperatures of 60–80°F will keep it quite comfortable, and it needs added humidity from misting and/or a humidifier, especially as the temperature climbs.

DON'T "DESERT" ME: Hot, dry air from a heating vent can be as upsetting to your schefflera as an icy wind, and either can cause it to drop its leaves.

▶ A peat-based potting mix with good drainage will make a happy potful for your umbrella plant's roots. Repot every year or two in the spring, increasing pot size until you reach a maximum manageable size. In subsequent years, refresh the top layer of your schefflera's potting soil when repotting is no longer practical.

FEED ME

▶ During the spring and summer, water your umbrella tree when the top inch of its potting soil is dry. While its lovely leaflets may droop if it gets thirsty, overwatering can make it sad and sulky. Water less often during the winter but attend to humidity when the heat is on in your home.

▶ Monthly feeding with a balanced fertilizer or a springtime serving of slow-release granules will keep your schefflera well nourished.

LOVE ME

Balance the base: Don't "overpot" your umbrella tree but do choose a hefty container to help balance its substantial, leafy top growth, which may extend to 8 feet tall and 4–5 feet wide.

Green and glossy: Your umbrella tree's broad leaflets are good at cleaning the air in your home of volatile organic compounds (VOCs) and other common pollutants. Keep them at peak performance and help your sprout absorb the light it needs by regularly spritzing its leaves and gently wiping them clean with a soft, damp cloth.

Velvet plant, purple passion
(Gynura aurantiaca)

A good choice for the plant parent with a passion for purple, velvet plant bears deep green, toothed leaves covered by downy purple hairs on lax, somewhat trailing stems that may stretch 8–20 inches long. A fast-growing plant that looks nice in a broad pot or hanging basket, velvet plant makes a handsome color companion for the smooth, multicolored leaves of calathea or prayer plant. Its purple presence contrasts attractively with bright green or white-variegated neighbors. Wherever you place it, your velvet plant's fuzzy leaves will invite you to pet it whenever you pass by.

Date I brought you home: _____

What I loved about you from the start: _____

Milestones in your growth: _____

HELP ME GROW

▶ Velvet plant needs moderate to bright lighting to keep its pretty colors and sturdy growth. In too little light, its stems will tend to stretch and new growth will be pale green.

▶ Average room temperatures (60–75°F) and moderate humidity will keep your velvet plant comfortable. The warmer its room, the greater its need for increased humidity.

DON'T MIST ME: Use a pebble tray or humidifier to maintain comfortable conditions for your velvet plant. Misting its fuzzy leaves can cause unsightly spots on the foliage.

▶ Good-quality potting soil will meet the needs of your velvet plant. Repot annually in spring until the plant's purple beauty fades.

FEED ME

▶ Water velvet plant with care, keeping its soil lightly and evenly moist but avoiding wetting its furry foliage. Let the top half inch of soil dry out between drinks but watch for wilting that indicates it's getting too thirsty.

▶ Feed your velvet plant every 2–3 weeks with a balanced fertilizer diluted to half strength. Cut back to monthly rations during the winter.

LOVE ME

Your little stinker: When your purple passion reaches maturity, it may bloom in spring, producing small orange-yellow flowers that have an odor most people find unappealing. Pinch off flowers before they open to encourage bushier growth and avoid their smell.

Forever young: Once a velvet plant has bloomed, it starts to decline. While you can pinch back the stem tips to keep your sprout from growing leggy and unattractive, it is easier to root cuttings taken from the stem tips and start with new, young plants than it is to keep a velvet plant older than 3 or 4 years looking nice.

Wax plant

(Hoya carnosa)

A leafy vine with clusters of fragrant flowers, wax plant has glossy, 3-inch-long leaves and blooms in spring and summer. Its long-lasting flowers are white to pale pink with red centers and their sweet fragrance tends to be more noticeable in the evening. Wax plant may stretch its vines over 10 feet long; this sprout needs parental support to help it climb to its full potential. A variegated form has leaves trimmed with creamy white. For spaces too snug for this vigorous viner, the smaller miniature wax plant (*Hoya bella*) bears similar flowers on a shorter vining plant.

Date I brought you home: _____

What I loved about you from the start: _____

Milestones in your growth: _____

HELP ME GROW

▶ Bright light is a must for wax plant to be able to produce its pretty blooms. Direct summer sun may be too much for its leaves, but a few hours of direct sun in winter are beneficial, and good, filtered light is called for the rest of the year.

▶ Let your wax plant vine in a room where temperatures range from 65–75°F and don't drop below 50°F in winter. In warmer conditions, humidity is important and your little hoya will appreciate regular misting as well as a pebble tray or humidifier for its comfort.

▶ Plant in a well-drained, peat-based potting mix. Repot in spring when your wax plant becomes crowded in its pot. Provide a trellis or stakes for your hoya to clamber up.

FEED ME

▶ From spring into fall, water enough to keep your wax plant's soil evenly moist, allowing the top half inch of soil to dry out between drinks. Water modestly in winter, sprinkling just enough to keep the soil from drying out completely.

▶ Feed your hoya every 2–3 weeks during the spring and summer with a flowering-plant fertilizer diluted to half strength. Feed once a month in winter.

LOVE ME

A *sensitive soul*: Your wax plant can be a bit touchy when it's preparing to flower and any upset can cause it to drop its buds. Do not move or repot a hoya when it has buds or flowers on it.

Don't pick the flowers: Wax plant's flower stalks (spurs) produce multiple flower clusters over the years. Let faded flowers drop off on their own or, if you can't bear to look at the spent blooms, carefully remove just the old flowers. Removing the spurs will reduce the number of flowers produced in future seasons.

Yucca

(Yucca elephantipes)

A sturdy brown stem crowned by rosettes of spiky leaves gives yucca exotic appeal. Yucca grows slowly to a height of 5–6 feet. Its deep green and glossy foliage may grow 1–2 feet long and has rough edges. Yucca makes a handsome floor plant for a bright, sunny location and can be a steady presence in your home without a lot of fuss or care. Yuccas grown outdoors bloom on 2-foot flower spikes produced from the centers of their leafy rosettes, but indoor-grown plants are unlikely to bloom.

Date I brought you home: _____

What I loved about you from the start: _____

Milestones in your growth: _____

HELP ME GROW

▶ Your yucca will enjoy bright light, including some direct sun. If you move your sprout from indoor lighting to a bright spot outdoors, make the relocation gradually to give it time to adjust.

▶ Your yucca is easygoing about temperature and will tolerate a range from 50–80°F. Fluctuations within that range won't trouble it, although it dislikes spending time in temperatures below 45°F.

ARID IS OKAY: Dry indoor air that would trouble many houseplants doesn't bother yucca, making it a great choice for a spot where you want a palmlike plant that isn't as fussy as an actual palm.

▶ Potting medium with a significant percentage of sand will provide the excellent drainage that your yucca's roots require. This sprout's upright posture and long-leaved rosettes can make your yucca top-heavy and it's proactive parenting to give it a weighty container to prevent it from tipping over easily. Repot in the spring when its roots become crowded in their container, usually every 2–3 years, until it reaches maximum manageable size. Refresh the top layer of potting soil annually thereafter.

FEED ME

▶ During the spring and into fall, water modestly, allowing the top 2 inches of soil to dry out between drinks. Water even less in the winter, especially if your yucca is in a cool location, keeping the potting mix from drying out completely. Overwatering, particularly during winter, poses a much greater risk to your yucca than drying out.

▶ Feed your yucca lightly, serving it a balanced fertilizer diluted to half strength every month in spring and summer. Pause feeding during the winter months.

LOVE ME

Off with its head: A yucca that grows too tall and tippy for its space in your home can be saved with decisive parental action: cut off its stem about midway in the spring. New growth will sprout from the stem just below the cut.

Not for Fido or Fluffy: All parts of yucca are toxic to pets. While your fur kids may not find your yucca particularly tempting, it's good practice to discourage curious nibblers from sampling any plant siblings.

ZZ plant

(Zamioculcas zamiifolia)

The 2- to 3-foot-tall upright stems of ZZ plant arch slightly to form an attractive vase-shaped plant clad in rows of glossy 2-inch leaves. Its light green to tan stems are slightly bulbous at the base, becoming slender as they stretch upward. An ideal adoptee for absentminded plant parents, ZZ plant, sometimes known as Zanzibar gem, is highly drought tolerant and accepting of low indoor humidity. Its orderly rows of leaves give it a fernlike appearance, but your ZZ can prosper in conditions no fern would tolerate. Displayed atop a pedestal or as a floor plant, your pretty ZZ plant will be a reliable and attractive accent plant in your home with a modest level of care.

Date I brought you home: _____

What I loved about you from the start: _____

Milestones in your growth: _____

HELP ME GROW

▶ Tolerance of a broad range of lighting is one of ZZ plant's many talents, and it can get by on relatively low light. But your little ZZ will grow and look its best in bright, indirect or filtered light. Full sun, however, can scorch its pretty leaves.

▶ Average to warm room temperatures (60–80°F) are in your ZZ plant's comfort zone. It will enjoy a cool rest period in the winter when lower light levels will cause its growth to slow for a few months. Dry indoor air doesn't trouble ZZ plant.

▶ Well-drained soil is a must for your ZZ plant. Fill its container with cactus potting mix or any potting medium amended with coarse sand. Repot every 2–3 years when its container becomes crowded.

FEED ME

▶ Your ZZ plant won't fuss if you fail to water it for a few weeks at a time. During the spring and summer, water only when the top 2 inches of its potting soil are dry, and even less often in winter. Too much water is much more of a danger to this unthirsty sprout.

SAD WHEN SOGGY: Yellowing leaves may signal that your ZZ plant is getting too much water or is sitting in soggy potting soil. Let things dry out and, if your baby doesn't seem to be recovering, check its roots for darkened, mushy root rot and trim such areas away before repotting in fresh soil.

▶ Feed your ZZ plant a light diet of balanced fertilizer diluted to half the recommended strength, serving it once a month in spring though late summer.

LOVE ME

Handle with care: ZZ plant's sap can cause skin irritation. Always wear gloves when repotting or handling it to prevent unpleasant conflicts with your sprout.

Keep me tidy: An occasional shower to remove dust from your ZZ plant's glossy foliage is welcome, although use care to avoid oversoaking its soil in the process. You can also wipe the leaves with a damp cloth, but this can be a lengthy process with this leafy plant.

More, please: You can easily increase your ZZ plant population by dividing its rhizomes in the spring when you repot it.

M

Madagascar dragon tree, 107

maidenhair fern, 117–118

Mammillaria spp., 84

Maranta leuconeura, 86, 171–172

mealybugs, 39

measuring spoons, 16

Meyer lemon, 97

micronutrients, 31

minerals, 24

miniature date palm, 102, 103

miniature wax plant, 206

misting techniques, 21

misting tools, 16

money tree, 134–135

monstera (*Monstera deliciosa*), 136–137

mother-in-law's tongue (snake plant), 181–182

mother-of-thousands (*Kalanchoe daigremontiana*), 133

mother-of-thousands (*Saxifraga stolonifera*), 160, 189–190

mother-of-thousands (*Tolmiea menziesii*), 159–160

moth orchid, 138–139

Musa spp., 64–65

Muscari spp., 79

Myers fern, 61

N

Narcissus cultivars, 77-78

Neoregella carolinae 'Tricolor,' 74

Nephrolepis exaltata, 70-71

nerve plant, 140–141

nitrogen, 31

Norfolk Island pine, 142–143

nutrients, 31

O

offsets (pups), 45

old lady cactus, 84

Oncidium spp., 146

orchids

    care and feeding of, 144–145

    cattleya, 145–146

    dancing lady, 146

    dendrobium, 146

    lady's slipper, 146

    moth, 138–139

    potting mix for, 23, 24

oxalis (*Oxalis* spp.), 179–180

P

potassium, 31

pot feet, 17

pothos, 44, 169–170

pots, 25–26

potting mixes, 22–25

powder puff cactus, 84

powdery mildew, 40

prayer plant, 86, 171–172

problem diagnosis

    care basics and, 35

    lighting issues, 19–20

    plant symptoms, 36–37

propagation, 42–45. *See also*
    specific plants

pruning techniques, 34. *See also*
    specific plants

pruning tools, 16

Pteris spp., 116

pups (offsets), 45

purple passion, 204–205

pygmy date palm, 102, 103

Q

Queen Victoria agave, 51

R

rabbit's foot fern, 118–119

rabbit tracks, 172

radiator plant, 155

radiators, 22

rainwater, 28

rat's tail cactus, 84

repotting techniques, 40–42

Rex begonia, 67

Rhapis excelsa, 150

ribbon fern, 116

robellini (miniature
    date palm), 103

root rot, 40

root symptoms, 37

rubber plant (*Ficus elastica*), 122

rubber plant (*Peperomia
    obtusifolia*), 155

S

sago palm, 173–174

Saintpaulia hybrids.
    See African violet

salt residue, 33–34

sand, 23

Sansevieria spp., 181–182

Saxifraga stolonifera, 160,
    189–190

scale insects, 39, 149

scarlet star, 175–176

scented geraniums, 177–178

V

velvet plant, 204–205

vermiculite, 23

W

watering cans, 15

watering techniques, 21, 27–29.
*See also specific
plants*

watermelon peperomia, 155

watermelon pilea (aluminum
plant), 161–162

wax plant, 206–207

weeping fig, 122

wellness checks, 34–35

whiteflies, 39

windowsills, 22

worm castings, 24

Y

yucca (*Yucca elephantipes*),
208–209

Z

Zamioculcas zamiifolia,
210–211

Zantedeschia hybrids, 77

Zanzibar gem (ZZ plant),
210–211

zebra plant (*Cryptanthus
zonatus*), 101

zebra plant (*Haworthia
fasciata*), 126–127

ZZ plant, 210–211

❧ MEET YOUR ❧
PLANT-PARENTING GUIDES

ABOUT THE AUTHOR

Deborah L. Martin has been sharing her love and knowledge of indoor and outdoor gardening for decades. A former extension agent in the USDA's urban gardening program, she has contributed to numerous books and magazines, including *The Complete Compost Gardening Guide*, *Rodale's Organic Life*, and *GROW: The Magazine of the Pennsylvania Horticultural Society*. When she's not gardening or writing, she manages the Bethlehem Farmers Market at Lehigh University in Pennsylvania.

ABOUT THE ILLUSTRATOR

Yu Kito Lee is an illustrator and motion designer based in Los Angeles. She draws inspiration from the tiny details of everyday life and exploring vibrant sceneries when she travels. When she's not drawing, you can find her out and about with her family, listening to live music, visiting museums, trying new food, reading, and traveling to faraway places.